THE REVENUE ACCELERATION FRAMEWORK

BRIAN,

I'M FOREVER GRATEFUL FOR YOUR VISION, SUPPORT, AND INSIGHTS.

Doug Davidoff

5/24

Brian,
I'm forever grateful
for your vision, support,
and insights

[illegible signature]
5/24

THE REVENUE ACCELERATION FRAMEWORK

A PROVEN ROADMAP TO TRANSFORM AND DYNAMICALLY GROW YOUR BUSINESS

DOUG DAVIDOFF

THE REVENUE ACCELERATION FRAMEWORK
A Proven Roadmap to Transform and Dynamically Grow Your Business

FIRST EDITION

ISBN 978-1-5445-3774-0 *Hardcover*
978-1-5445-3775-7 *Paperback*
978-1-5445-3776-4 *Ebook*

To Mom & Dad, for giving me the space to learn to be myself.

To Dani, Drew, & Dylan for inspiring me to continue to dream.

CONTENTS

INTRODUCTION

THE BUSINESS WORLD HAS CHANGED.

In 1994, my mom, dad, brother, and I started VALU Travel Marketing, a "consultium" that was a mix of a franchise, consulting company, and a consortium for travel agencies. We were in the space because my parents owned a travel agency, were well-known in the industry, and had worked as direct consultants with travel agencies for years.

To fund the business, my parents took out a second mortgage on their house, we raised a small amount of money from friends and colleagues who liked our business idea, and my brother and I each contributed some money. I left my job as a regional sales manager for The Hertz Corporation to become the VP of Sales for VALU. We had big goals and big expectations, and people in the industry voiced their support.

They said, "What a great idea!" "Once you've gotten started, we definitely want to work with you." All that talk turned out to be just that—talk.

The first thing we did was print five thousand informational packets that outlined our business, who we were, why we were different and highlighted the services we would provide (today we call it a website). Our primary business development strategy was to choose a city, go there on Tuesday morning, run a free seminar (webinars didn't exist back then) on how to generate more business and profit for their travel agency, then set up meetings with those who attended or had expressed interest in attending. I was the salesperson, so I would travel with my mom who ran the seminar at the beginning of the week. I'd spend the rest of the week in sales calls, making additional presentations and attempting to close business.

We were about four and a half months in when we decided to approach the West Coast. Since I love the Phoenix area and a lot of people there knew of my parents, I suggested we start off with two weeks in Phoenix, Arizona. We were pretty confident when we scheduled our time that everything would be "Skittles and rainbows."

Sure enough, the turnout for the seminar was great, with approximately 50 people in attendance. But by my fifth sales call, I realized things weren't working out as we expected. Every meeting I had, every follow-up with someone from the seminar, was a mixture of ambivalent sounds. "Wow. This is really great. Definitely something we'll consider at a future time." "No, no, you're really great. This is really interesting. But the timing isn't right..."

Although few ever told us "no," even fewer were telling us "yes," and we were spending much more money than we were making. I had left a fairly well-paying job, and this was not the result I had been expecting.

After one particularly frustrating meeting, I pulled into a McDonald's drive-through to get lunch. I got my order, and sat in my car, eating a Quarter Pounder with cheese while talking to my brother, mom, and dad, who were back in the office and waiting for a progress report. I had to tell them, "This isn't working." We made the decision to cut the trip short and for me to fly home.

I hung up the phone and began to cry there in the McDonald's parking lot. *Holy shit, what were we gonna do?* My parents had taken out a second mortgage. How were we going to go back to friends and family who'd invested money in us and believed in us and say, "Nevermind"?

After I returned home that Saturday morning, my family convened in the office and started brainstorming ideas on flip charts (whiteboards were rare back then). It quickly became clear that we had a very strong point of view, an innovative perspective, but we were positioning ourselves, selling ourselves, and highlighting the features and benefits of our business exactly the same as everyone else in the industry. We firmly believed we had a new idea, but we were just not making a strong case for change to our potential clients and competitors. We weren't asking ourselves the right questions. It wasn't, "How do we beat the competition at their game?" We needed to ask, "What can we do differently… What's our game?"

As the sales and marketing experts of today would say, we were "out of alignment." We had a new business and a new approach to the travel industry, but we were marketing it just like our status quo competitors. What we did was create a lot of confusion, and when there's confusion, people don't change. So, over that weekend at the office, my family made our new game plan.

If we were to succeed with VALU, we had to define our game, what its parameters were, and then we had to play that game. It can be nerve-wracking when you don't have the certainty of success, when you're one of the first to step off the beaten path, but this was a risk we took to define our game and play it right. Two weeks after the lukewarm response in Phoenix, we had completely repositioned everything, including the seminar. The change to the seminar was simple; we started charging for admission.

We called it the $19 seminar series. The added cost increased attendees' incentive to actually attend. Our no-show rate went from 40–60 percent to less than 10 percent. The seminar was no longer something someone might show up to if they maybe had a free hour; it cost something, and that made it an investment and an event to plan for. It might not seem like a big deal nowadays, but we'd switched from a free program to a fee'd program during a time when people didn't charge for those types of seminars. We had taken a gamble because we needed to get ourselves out of the status quo we had marketed ourselves into. And it worked.

Now, I'm not going to say the business was a home run or that we were suddenly an overnight success. We still faced the same problem that 99 percent of small businesses had—we weren't adequately capitalized to achieve everything we wanted with the venture—but we did get ourselves out of the red and onto a solid ground of profitability. My parents were able to pay back their loan, and we eventually sold the company to a subsidiary of American Express. That was the end of VALU Travel Marketing, and those early experiences with VALU became some of the most important lessons that guided me through the next 20 years of my career. And all those years of accumulated experiences finally culminated into this book.

THE MORE THINGS CHANGE, THE MORE THINGS STAY THE SAME (UNFORTUNATELY)

As you read through this book, you may notice that I use terms like "marketing," "sales," and "customer success" interchangeably. Of course, the specific tactics and intricacies of each term do differ from the next, but in this book, I am more interested in exploring marketing, sales, and customer success through the lens of the Revenue Acceleration Framework™. Within the Framework, they are all parts of a greater whole.

With that in mind, let's start this section off with a hypothetical: Imagine Rip Van Winkle is the VP of a company in 1978. Just like in the original story, he falls asleep and wakes up in modern day. If he walked into any business today, he'd be beside himself, absolutely baffled by the way things work.

He'd go into the accounting department, and he'd be looking for the green lamps and paper and manual ledgers. He'd walk into operations and—holy cow!—everything is just indecipherable. He'd walk into the marketing department, and he'd ask, "Where do you keep your brochures? What's that? What the hell is an email?" Finally, he'd walk over to the sales side, pop his head through the door, and breathe a sigh of relief. "Now, that's more like it!"

Don't get me wrong. Sales has changed since 1978, just not by much. All of the accouterments have changed. We're using cell phones and personal computers. We've got CRM software. We're using different stuff, but sales is still fundamentally the same. It's salespeople pounding numbers—"spraying and praying." Every other aspect of business has changed fundamentally, from accounting to manufacturing. Sales has changed in degree, but it's fundamentally the same. For the vast, vast majority of businesses, the way they go to market hasn't changed much. If you were to go back and compare the copy of magazine articles of the 1970s with the blog posts of the 2010s, would you be able to tell the difference?

By and large, the way businesses are going to market has changed but not transformed. Meanwhile, everything around the go-to-market approach has transformed. According to Daniel H. Pink in his 2013 YouTube video "7 Questions in 10 Minutes—The New World of Sales & Selling," "It's that the changes in sales have been in 'degree' when they need to be in 'kind.'" That isn't to say companies aren't trying to make those necessary changes. If anything, I'd say the backend of marketing and sales has changed dramatically in recent years. We live in this new world where buzzwords are introduced and discarded all the time, and companies today are investing more money than ever in order to play the new games. But as the father of disruptive innovation, Clayton Christensen, once said: "In business strategy, the new game begins before the old game is over."

That is where we find ourselves in sales—on the precipice of the old game, which still has its hooks in us, as we're trying to learn the parameters of a new game. As an example, this is what companies are trying to do when they're spending large amounts of money on tech in marketing. They know the change is coming, and the new game has already started. But even as they undergo this digital transformation, too many of these companies fail to transform their *approach* to the game. The companies that struggle to gain traction after switching to the new game are the companies that are still trying to play the new game by the old rules.

Consider this: the "inbound marketing" movement that began back in 2005 initiated a fundamental change in how companies went about generating leads, using websites, blog posts, etcetera. Strangely, even with all the money being saved on printing and paper, marketing organizations were spending more money than ever before. Despite all of these investments designed to "increase efficiency," the cost of customer acquisition kept rising as the sales cycles continued to get longer.

MORE FOR THE SQUEEZE

The dominant approach to business today is still more, more, more. Even outside of business, we're obsessed with speed. But we're actually conflating size with scale and speed with velocity. Speed is a measurement of how fast we're going, but it's directionless. Velocity is a measurement of progress. It doesn't matter how fast you're going if you don't get to your destination. Most businesses are already operating at max capacity. They're going as fast as they can. So, the solution is not to blindly spend more money to do more. That's not sustainable. Instead, businesses should be asking how they can gain more from what they're already putting forth. How do you get more juice for the squeeze?

Let's go back to the previous, real-world example. Companies sink money into tech as a means of achieving growth. Growth is a common goal of any company, but growth is not equal to scale. Scale is generating growth with more predictability at a lower unit cost—capturing more for less. But what companies end up doing when they fixate on more, more, more is they end up capturing more for more.

So much of the underlying performance of businesses today depends on value extraction far more than value creation. What technology has done is increase the volume of what we can do. We're sending a billion emails with the effort it used to take to write one letter. We're capturing more not because we've become stronger or more efficient, but because we're simply doing more. And the cost of acquisition is still increasing while all this "growth" is being achieved.

You might be thinking, *If it still works, it can't be that inefficient.*

The thing is, if you jumped off of an 80-story building, you could convince yourself you're flying for the first 79 floors.

And when it comes to growth without scale, the ratio hasn't changed; the price has just gone up. When people get stuck doing more with more instead of more with less, they end up with twice the risk and only a fraction of the results they should be getting. That juice is not worth the squeeze!

THE REVENUE ACCELERATION FRAMEWORK AND BASEBALL

In my experience working with growth teams, I've observed that one of the biggest flaws that puts a drag on their efforts is the pursuit of the "right answer" when the most valuable thing we can do is to ask the better questions. That's why I wrote this book, to enable you to ask those better questions. I'll share my insight on why good companies don't hit their potential, while others do. There is often a chasm between the intent of a growth strategy and the execution, performance, and result of said strategy, and I'll explain why that happens and how the Revenue Acceleration Framework can help you close that chasm for your own business.

This is a book of questions and explanations, but it isn't a textbook of solutions; this book is a framework that can show you if you're on course for your own path, because no two paths are the same. In fact, finding your own growth path is a lot like batting in baseball.

In the past, I coached junior college baseball for three years, and in two of those years, our offense ranked in the top 20 in the United States. I'm passionate about the sport, and there's a lot of fantastic analogies between baseball and business growth. The most relevant comparison I can make here is between your growth path and the swing path. In baseball, every batter has a different batting stance. Every athlete is working with different biomechanics, right? There's a science to hitting a baseball, which leads to what baseball insiders like to call the "swing path." The swing path is basically the three key points in the swing that can maximize the probability of hitting the ball squarely. Every batter is different, and every pitch is different. So, although every pitch and every swing is different, the underlying swing path is consistent.

Hitting a baseball is a dynamic activity; the same can be said for growing a business. That's why fixating on the "right answer" is not actually the way to find your growth path. This book will get you to ask better questions and make better observations. It's going to help you identify the critical inflection points of your own growth path, a framework that can increase the probability of success for your business.

Because that's what the Revenue Acceleration Framework is all about: breaking down the key components of a growth path. You may not be running a company like HubSpot, Salesforce, Microsoft, The Four Seasons, Johnson & Johnson, The Grateful Dead, or Procter & Gamble, but there's always an underlying commonality for these successful companies, a framework, which I will share with you. Once you can identify the framework and the right questions to ask, you can tailor the contents of this book to your own growth path and achieve your business goals.

WHY THIS BOOK?

In the past decades, I've gotten hands-on with the go-to-market and growth strategies of thousands of mid-market businesses. The work I did for 25 of those companies contributed to these companies raising, funding, and selling liquidity for nearly $2 billion total. I've been there for the beginning, middle, and end of countless businesses' journeys of success. I've seen the difference in framework between companies that achieved success and those that didn't.

All too often, I've encountered companies who were aspiring to walk the growth path of GE, Apple, or Amazon. But most businesses are not GE. GE has the ability to issue billions of dollars of bonds at insanely low-interest rates. The game they're playing is fundamentally different than the game a mid-market company is playing. I'm not saying there's nothing to be learned from the success stories of these behemoth businesses, but there's far more to be gained from understanding the framework of success than emulating every detail of their game.

Through a combination of industry experience and added research, a pattern emerged from these success stories, a throughline for all these top-performing companies. I began to see a framework for revenue acceleration. The growth path of these major companies reflected this framework, even if they weren't aware of it. This is the simple reason why this book exists—to enable businesses to consciously use the Revenue Acceleration Framework, rather than stumble upon it by chance.

This is not an instruction manual or a book of answers. I wrote this book to share my experiences, and what you make of this resource is up to you. My decades of field research and data are here. The Revenue Acceleration Framework is here. Do what you will—the choice is yours.

PART I

PREPARING TO WIN

CHAPTER 1

THE REVENUE ACCELERATION MANIFESTO

JACK WELCH, CEO OF GE THAT LED THE COMPANY DURING THEIR high growth days of the 1980s and 90s, once famously said, "If the rate of change on the outside exceeds the rate of change on the inside, the end is near." He's also well known for being a bit of a dick, but his words still ring true for anyone who's trying to do business in the long term. To stay relevant, you have to change.

For most people, the rate of change outside their organization is far, far greater than the rate of change within their organization. The world around them is changing much faster than they are. Like Rip Van Winkle, there are businesses in every industry that get comfortable, get complacent, and fall asleep in the innovation department, only to wake up and find themselves lost in an unfamiliar world. Companies are investing in technology to enable sales and marketing departments to do more with less. And yet, the cost of customer acquisition is going up. That isn't doing more with less; that's doing more with more.

One of the catchphrases commonly touted about inbound marketing was that this new, revolutionary strategy enabled you to "compete on the size of your brain, not the size of your wallet." But take a good look at any market today; the split of rewards has only increased in favor of the largest players, the ones who can afford to spend more to earn more.

Over the past three years, the average number of technology applications used by businesses has more than tripled; yet simultaneously, companies are hiring more salespeople than ever before, especially growth companies. This is all despite the popular opinion in the past decade that technology was going to greatly displace salespeople. We're doing these new things, forming these new categories, and trying all these new methodologies. But these "innovations" aren't fundamentally changing the horizontals and verticals of business. Companies—or, more accurately, their employees—are working harder, doing more, spending more, and taking more risks. And the expenditure of all of that blind energy is degrading just about every underlying measurement on the use of capital.

The rise in tech spend and the unprecedented growth in new sales hires reveals a deeper flaw in the dominant, legacy approach to sales and marketing: it is more evident than ever before that businesses aren't growing effectively, and only the biggest corporations can even afford to see substantial growth. What most companies are doing is not sustainable nor sufficient enough to retain their relevance against their competitors who might outpace them in sheer numbers alone. A company nowadays needs a framework that won't just let them survive, but thrive; and to attain that framework, a company must be willing to embrace change.

THE REVENUE ACCELERATION MANIFESTO

While I may have ended the Introduction by saying, "The choice is yours," the reality is that some things won't be a choice. If you want to win the game, if you want the real payoff of growing your business, then change is not a choice. What is a choice is what you make of the information I provide in this book. The Revenue Acceleration Framework is a choice. It is by no means the only path to success, because every winner has a different strategy to victory. But every victory is the same: it's about scoring more than your opponents. It's about getting more for the squeeze, and it's about changing course ahead of the curve.

Change is not a choice; it is the only option outside of obsoletion.

THE FIVE TRENDS THAT DETERMINE THE WINNERS

I've discovered five major trends of today's game that can reliably determine its leading players. In today's game, there are plenty of businesses that are able to change and succeed without consciously paying attention to their winning strategies. They play in accordance with the five trends. Whether knowingly or not, the winners of today's market are aligning with these trends to achieve the growth in revenue that they do. By becoming conscious of the framework, you can adjust your decision-making strategies and generate greater traction and impact from the actions and efforts you are already taking.

Some of these trends are successful strategies of the winners, while other trends are flaws of companies that fell short of the competition. But all five trends are a reflection of how today's winners embrace effective change and differentiate themselves as a cut above the rest.

1ST TREND: MARKETS ARE NOISIER, AND BUYERS ARE MORE CONFUSED

According to information published by Gartner, a technological and research firm, 55 percent of consumers surveyed say they encounter an "overwhelming amount of trustworthy information." But 44 percent of consumers also struggle with the fact that the information supplied by various companies all appear to be trustworthy, yet highly contradictory. Eighty-nine percent of buyers feel that the information they encounter as part of making a purchase decision is of high quality, and customers today spend, on average, 15 percent of their purchasing time just trying to reconcile the conflicting information presented by competitors.

The point is that being competitive is not enough to win. In poker terms, the fish have left the game, and everybody left at the table is a pro.

It is no longer enough to have a "strong" sales process or a "powerful" message. It's not enough to be loud. You've got to be clever and break through the noise. In the future, insight will be the greater differentiator between the winners and losers, not sheer competitiveness.

2ND TREND: SELLERS ARE LESS PRESENT

When I entered the world of sales in the late 80s, it was a whole different game being played. It used to be that if a salesperson was good enough, they would go straight to the final decision-maker. If they could influence that decision-maker well enough, they could make the sale.

Nowadays, and as often as not, business has no decision-makers. The way initiatives get triggered and managed is more complex than ever, and sellers are less present at critical points along the buying journey. Consensus is also becoming the dominant form of decision-making on the part of companies.

There is a popular statistic in circulation which claims that consumers are two-thirds of the way through their buying journey before they're open to talking to a salesperson. However, based on research done by Aberdeen and by Challenger Inc., 73 percent of buyers are actually willing to meet with salespeople earlier than the consideration phase—so, earlier than the decision-making phase. If salespeople would help the buyer define their problems and needs, share insights about their sales category or their competitors, and provide objective information that would help the buyer frame their decisions, there would still be a clear place for salespeople in the decision-making process.

The point of highest value for sales and marketing is in what I would refer to as the problem identification phase. Yet, additional research from Challenger Inc. shows that sellers only participate 11 percent of the time in the problem identification phase. So, the selling and marketing organizations are absent in the phase of the decision process where they retain most of their relevance.

This is what I mean when I say, "Sellers are less present." It's not that marketing and sales are getting phased out by reluctant buyers. The buyers *want* sellers there at the point of highest value, at the problem identification phase, but a vast majority of sellers just aren't meeting them there.

3RD TREND: CONSENSUS-BASED DECISION-MAKING IS THE DOMINANT BUYING STYLE

When talking about the presence of sellers I already kind of inferred this point, but it deserves its own spot on the list: Consensus-based decision-making is becoming the dominant buying style in today's markets. If you take a look at who's directly involved in making decisions for B2B purchases, the number of direct influencers has increased by 25 percent, growing from an average of 5.4 to an average of 6.8 direct influencers, all with different and often conflicting priorities and objectives.

According to information published in *The JOLT Effect*, authors Matt Dixon and Ted Mckenna show that with the rise in direct influencers, 40 to 60 percent of B2B processes nowadays end up in a stalemate. No decision gets made. It used to be that you only had to compete within your category. So, if I sold HR services, I competed with other HR services. If I sold printing, I competed with other printers. But then the 2009 recession happened, and by the time 2010 rolled around, the whole idea of discretionary funding had just up and left. And it never really came back.

Nowadays, you are competing for a piece of the overall budget. In many ways, the easy problems have been solved for buyers, and what's left are the problems and needs that everybody has their own solution for. It's no longer a question of "Which HR system are we gonna invest in?" It's become a question of "Do we even want an HR system? What about a supply chain system? What about something else?"

The problems and needs we're dealing with today are more complex and nuanced than ever before. Buyers are overwhelmed, and companies are overwhelmed. As people rely more and more on consensus decision-making, safety becomes the default choice. Buyers in every market are saying, "I'll go with the safest option since I don't know what the hell

I'm doing." This pushes buyers and companies alike further and further into a status quo because whatever is familiar always seems safer. If you talk to seller organizations or individual salespeople, they'll tell you that the problem isn't buyers saying, "No." The problem is buyers saying, "I don't know."

4TH TREND: COMPANIES LACK THE RIGHT DATA (AND THE RIGHT QUESTIONS)

There's an old phrase that goes, "What gets measured gets done." But what people always forget to mention is that you better be careful what you measure and how you measure it. A good case of this would be when Howard Schultz first stepped down as CEO of Starbucks. This happened in the early 2000s, and when Schultz retired, he was replaced by executives who viewed things far more through an operations & efficiency lens. As they started looking at the data, they identified the cost of having fresh beans in the store as a place to reduce operational expenses. They tested centralizing the roasting and freeze-drying the beans. They found that not only did this increase efficiencies and reduce costs; they also found that the beans stayed fresher and in taste tests, the coffee tasted better. For a period of time, the performance at Starbucks improved.

But then, as more and more Starbucks locations transitioned to stocking only freeze-dried beans, the coffee shops no longer had that fresh coffee smell. Nobody was consciously thinking, "I'm going to Starbucks because it smells like coffee." But the smell was a part of the buyer's experience. How were the freeze-dried beans going to improve the buyer's experience? That was an important question the operators forgot to answer in their quest for cheaper beans. It was some years before Starbucks really started seeing a downturn, but it was a significant and steep enough downturn that another major transformation of the storefront operations was called in. When Schultz returned as the CEO, Starbucks underwent another series of changes to get back to where it'd been in the early 2000s. It never quite reached its peak again, although it certainly got back to being very successful.

One of the major misconceptions in business is the idea that tomorrow's results will tell you if today's decision was good or bad. In reality, it's going to take quite some time for you to know the impact of your decisions. The results that you're getting today are driven by decisions that you made long before yesterday. To truly scale a business, to generate more juice for the squeeze, you have to ask the right questions and have the right data in hand to make the right decisions.

It turns out that even in our modern age of technology, data quality and accuracy are the top two areas of concern surrounding most companies' decision-making processes. What I find is that companies today are overwhelmed by the amount of data available to them. CRM is filled with data. Even when there is no CRM, there's far more information than anybody knows what to do with, but there's no structure to the data. In other words, the data is dirty.

When you don't know what information and which sources you can rely on (or, more importantly, which ones you can't), you end up taking a whole lot of time getting what you need out of the slog of information. By the time you've wrangled the data into something useful, it's already less valuable and less relevant because time has passed and there's now more up-to-date data to be processed, sifted through, and messed with.

It's not even that companies can't answer the important questions because of a lack of data-handling capabilities. I'm sure most companies already have their crazy Rube Goldberg machines ready to gather and sort through the avalanche of data at their disposal. The real problem is that companies aren't asking the right questions. When companies don't ask the right questions, the data becomes meaningless. Company insight becomes harder to build up to make quick, effective decisions. The data continues to pile up. Quantity trumps quality, and as the quality continues to atrophy, it leads to bad decision-making.

5TH TREND: SALES, MARKETING, AND CUSTOMER SUCCESS ARE STUMPED BY FRICTION

The fifth trend I often see, which is another problem in most sales and marketing organizations, is that they're operating on quicksand. To so many companies, it's all about more, more, more, and faster, faster, faster. But from a firsthand analysis, I've routinely seen results where these speedy sales and marketing organizations are producing somewhere between one-half and two-thirds of what they could be producing.

The average salesperson spends approximately 30 percent of their time actually selling, and they spend roughly 40 percent of their time dealing with administrative tasks. Every time a salesperson is having to do an administrative task, it creates friction. I call it the friction tax. When two systems aren't communicating correctly, and someone has to manage what someone else put into an Excel spreadsheet and then someone *else* has to manipulate it...all of that raises the friction tax. Everything takes a little bit longer and is a little bit more difficult than it should be. More resources and effort are required to work through these points of friction. It slowly adds up until you're left with individual salespeople and whole organizations underperforming tremendously, despite how "fast" everything is operating.

GOOD ENOUGH ISN'T ENOUGH ANYMORE

Most companies operate in the good zone, but things are fundamentally changing in the modern era of marketing and commerce, and the returns within the good zone are shrinking every day. The Amazons of the world are devouring that space. Technology combined with size enables them to do things that smaller, mid-market companies can't do. Today, you can't afford to operate in the good zone; it's just not good enough.

The shrinking good zone isn't just impacting small businesses, either. Look at the Dow Jones Industrial Index. It is representative of the 30 largest, most successful, most dominant companies to currently exist. In the past two decades, a third of the companies in the Dow have been removed and ten new companies have been added—including several newcomers which, for all practical purposes, didn't even exist two decades ago. For big and small players alike, there's a new game to play, and winning that game requires a new mindset and new approach to revenue, growth, and competition.

The first key shift in mindset should happen between speed and velocity. Speed is a measurement of how fast you're moving, but velocity measures how quickly you progress toward a specific point. In the old game, it was good enough to focus on speed. Today, the game is much more nuanced, and the dynamic of the game requires more than speed to get the job done. It is no longer just a quantity and numbers game, but a directional game too.

Another shift comes from utilizing big data to little data. In her book, *Thinking In Bets*, author Annie Duke explains that outcomes are determined by two variables: decision quality and luck. As I mentioned earlier, you can't control your luck. The only variable that businesses can directly impact is decision quality, and the primary value of data in modern markets is to improve a company's decision qualities. Yesterday's data was about giving you an overview of everything, an answer to everything. Today's data is about getting you to ask better questions and operate under better hypotheses.

The third shift is moving away from bloated tech. This is what I call the shift away from redundant horizontal tech stacks to tight, purposeful vertical tech stacks. Tech is great, but often bloated. More tech does not equal a better system of solutions. When people carelessly bring in technology to address friction, all these conflicting applications create even more friction and problems than they eliminate. Basically, the simpler the tech stack that can get the job done, the better.

The next shift happens between efficiency and vectors. Don't get me wrong, efficiency is great. In fact, getting more for the squeeze can seem like a simple matter of efficiency. But if we only fixate on "efficiency" as an answer, we would be doing no better than the companies who rely on "technology" or "speed" as an answer. In the 1980s, efficiency was a great talking point for manufacturers who stuck to efficiency as their universal solution for growth. The funny thing was, as these manufacturers became more and more efficient, they lost more and more money. They were so focused on efficiency that they didn't take into account the constraints and bottlenecks that would make their efficiency ineffective. Efficiency is all about speed, and, again, you need to move away from speed and toward velocity, toward progress and throughput. Today's game is not just about efficiency. It's about aligning your vectors, and orchestrating all of the main contributing elements to achieve great outcomes.

This leads us to another important shift, the shift away from silos and toward orchestrated action. Orchestrated action is about having the ability to orchestrate multiple dimensions and dynamics to produce greater throughput. When it comes to orchestrated action and growth, there are three ways businesses go about it: the old way, the new way, and the right way.

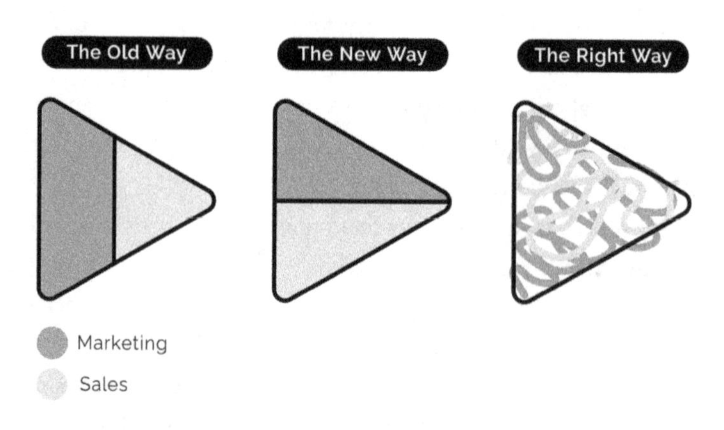

The old way put marketing first, then sales. This is how it used to be done: marketing would set up sales, and sales would close the deal. The new way is what a lot of mid-market companies are trying to do, where they make marketing and sales work parallel to each other. But the real right way to orchestrate marketing and sales is to integrate them.

The last mindset shift we'll cover here is the shift away from behavioral thinking and toward systems and design thinking. Historically, sales and marketing were approached as behavioral departments. But the winners of today and tomorrow are going to excel at system and design thinking. To better understand the importance of this shift toward systems and designs, we can refer to the philosophy of management expert W. Edwards Deming, the creator of the 14 points of total quality management. According to Deming, "Every system is perfectly designed to get the result that it does." To achieve different results, you would need to change the system. Focusing on individual behaviors only leads to diminishing impact and diminishing effect of change. If you want to set a different destination, a different velocity of growth, you need to change the direction and design of the system your business is operating in.

When we talk about shifts in mindset, it's all about moving away from outdated modes of thought which are residuals of the old games, games that we are no longer playing. A correct shift in mindset moves us away from blindly "doing more," and enables us to become more aware of the efficacy of what we're already doing. The biggest winners in growth and revenue acceleration are the businesses that are able to manage and eliminate friction from their already existing framework.

WHY I LIKE FRAMEWORKS

By now, you can probably tell I'm a big fan of frameworks, and that's because a framework is like a universal translator of productivity; it keeps everyone moving in the same direction and oriented toward the same fundamental goals.

Part of the problem in modern-day sales and marketing is that there are so many different methodologies to choose from. There's no end to terms like strategy, demand, generation, inbound marketing, outbound marketing…and they all mean very different things to different people. When words don't mean the same thing to everyone, it only creates an illusion of alignment. People think they're on the same page, but they aren't. This leads to friction, redundancy, and a constant desire to fall back on the status quo because the starting line seems to be the only place where everybody is facing the same direction.

That's why I'm a fan of frameworks. The Revenue Acceleration Framework is a foundation that any business can build upon with any method, category, strategy, or approach. It provides a fundamental structure to ensure that everybody is actually in alignment and the business isn't running in circles or in opposite directions. The Framework is also diagnostic. There is a prescriptive element to the Framework that can help identify root problems, create opportunities for change, and generate more juice for the squeeze.

THE DIFFERENCE BETWEEN SPEED AND VELOCITY

The Navy Seals has a simple mantra that goes: Slow is smooth. Smooth is fast. The business world is addicted to fast; it's obsessed with gaining more speed without a sense of direction, or velocity. But speed without velocity is just empty miles. Improvement without structure is unsustainable. This is how change initiatives fail.

Anybody who's serious about growing a business is already familiar with the buzzwords of "continuous and sustained improvement." But not everybody knows how to set up a structure of prioritization or schema to make it happen. Any change initiative that lacks structure will inevitably fall into the chasm between the strategy of a company and its execution, widening the distance between intended and actual performance.

When there is no structure in place for initiatives, people automatically sort their to-do list into "now" and "later." As we'll discuss more in a later chapter, not every task belongs in the same zone of execution. There's the immediate urgency of zone one and the abstract goals of zone three, but what a lot of companies lack is zone two, the crucial middle step. Zone two is the bridge that connects and lends structure to the otherwise detached zones one and three.

Whenever improvements exist to be made or problems exist to be solved, the first question we should be asking is: Which zone does it belong in? Only with deliberate, structured intent can you build a base of continuous and sustained improvement for your business.

TIPS AND TAKEAWAYS

In Chapter 1, we covered the need for change and the obstacles to change. To put this information into practice for your business, it is important to:

- Be conscious of the five trends that determine winners,
- Shift from old, outdated mindsets to new, effective mindsets,
- Overcome the inertia of the status quo and the "good enough" zone,
- Stop fixating on answers,
- And start asking the right questions.

Today, change is no longer a choice. As new companies go to market every minute and we become more and more inundated with the data at our fingertips, we can no longer rely on excess spending of resources—time, money, labor—to stay ahead of competitors. More is not enough. Good is not enough. If the rate of change outside surpasses the rate at which your organization changes internally, you will lose the game.

If victory is your destination, then change is your obligation, and the Revenue Acceleration Framework is fundamental to your winning strategy.

CHAPTER 2

REVENUE OPERATIONS

FRANKLIN LOGISTICS (NAME CHANGED FOR LEGAL PURPOSES) WAS a company that had experienced years of growth, but found itself in a place where growth no longer appeared sustainable. Revenues weren't going down, but they weren't going up either. Costs were increasing and the turnover of existing customers was increasing too. Even more worryingly, the company was discovering the challenges that were brought on by the very nature of its success.

Over their previous years of growth, they'd gone from an 80-million-dollar chemical logistics company to an approximately 150-million-dollar integrated logistics company. They were now providing asset and non-asset solutions, as well as strategic logistic services. The size and type of companies that they needed to win to sustain their success and the competitors that they needed to beat to win those customers had all changed drastically, and they couldn't experience the rates they'd grown used to.

The people at Franklin Logistics realized that what they'd done to get to where they were was not enough to get them to where they wanted to be. What follows is the story of how we worked with the company to enable a level of success they had thought was no longer possible.

We began by helping them assess their existing market, as well as their sales team and overall sales strategy. What we found was something I see regularly when working with growth-focused mid-market and small companies. The reality of their stagnation was that they had completely outgrown their systems and structures.

They needed a transformation.

Initially, the senior team balked at the idea. "Who has time for a total transformation?" they asked. "We're already a successful company, so we just need to adjust or pivot a bit."

However, a transformation doesn't need to take more time or resources than the other strategy of maintaining the status quo while making adjustments. As we explained to the senior team, in many ways, a transformation would take less overall effort and would involve less risk.

"How could that be?" they asked. We pointed out that the amount of energy, effort, and invested resources it would take to continue executing without a strong structure and systems would generate significant disruption, friction, and costs. Their underlying problem of operating upon a weakened structure was having to face greater and greater uncertainty and managing more and more variance.

Over the roughly five-year period that we worked with them, Franklin Logistics tripled their revenue while increasing revenue per rep by almost 20 percent. Gross margins increased by 17 percent and profits were 5 times what they were before while the company was still reinvesting profits in their business at a higher rate than industry norms.

How did we enable such a drastic transformation for Franklin Logistics? How was the company able to not just sustain its performance, but once again see progress in its revenue growth journey?

It was a matter of fixing the plumbing.

GREAT IDEAS, POOR PLUMBING

I've always loved great ideas. For the first part of my business career, I was an idea guy. I believed that the best idea would win the game. Over time, as I developed my theory of the Framework and dug further into the go-to-market strategy of the companies I worked with, I discovered that the biggest companies often weren't the ones with the best ideas. I found that the companies they were "beating" typically had ideas just as good, and it wasn't at all unusual that they had better ideas.

You might roll your eyes and think, "Of course!" Sure, this isn't a revelation for those of us who've been in business long enough to know it's not a simple meritocracy. Success is also about luck and the ability to catch the right opportunities at the right time, too. *How* you market is just as vital as *what* you market. But at the time, very early in my career, I was stunned by this truth. I was disappointed.

Many people outside of the industry will still look at a big brand and think, "Wow, that's a company that has its act together! They must be smarter than everybody else. I can't wait to work with and buy from them." And when I started working with larger companies, I realized that the air of exclusive excellence surrounding big brands was a complete farce. They're definitely not smarter than the smaller companies. More often than not, I found the smaller companies were actually the smarter ones with the better ideas.

I started looking closely at the real difference between the big-brand winners and the losers—the companies that didn't have the stories of success but actually had the receipts. They had the goods, but they didn't have the market. And that's when it clicked. A good idea or a good strategy is nothing without the plumbing to bring it into reality and sustain it.

Plenty of businesses have good ideas, but so many of them stumble over that crucial step. Why?

Chances are, your business has its receipts. It's got great ideas, but that isn't enough. When you're aiming for your revenue and growth objectives, you need to be able to answer a very important question: How are you going to unlock the potential that your company has? How are you going to strategize and execute those great ideas? This is the difference that I'm getting at between companies that succeed and companies that can only tread water. It's about the backend, underlying operations. It's about plumbing.

One of my favorite quotes of all time came from the mind of General

Omar Bradley: "Amateurs talk strategy. Professionals talk logistics." Now, what does that mean in terms of plumbing?

We can think about plumbing as just another form of logistics. It's a physical supply chain, a system that gets the right things at the right time into the right place. Sustaining good plumbing can be the difference between a hot shower and flooding in the basement. Plumbing is all about the myriad of wiring controls in the walls; it's the backend of how good ideas get carried through and supported and executed in an organization.

WHAT IS REVENUE OPERATIONS?

Formally, revenue operations is the strategic coordination of all market-facing, revenue-oriented systems, processes, and activities designed to increase velocity, optimize throughput, and reduce friction to solve for the customer and achieve revenue objectives.

Simply put, revenue operations is about getting more juice for the squeeze by managing friction and reducing complexity. Revenue operations are successful when revenue grows at a lower cost. This is the real underlying metric that should be focused on. Does it cost me relatively less to achieve revenue objectives? Can I get more revenue with less effort?

And how do great ideas and strategic execution tie into revenue operations?

Let's answer that question with another truth of the current market climate. I recently did a Google search on sales and marketing or when browsing the "Business" aisles of my local bookstore, I found so many titles on branding, on storytelling, on sales strategy. And when people talk about sales strategy, they are talking about what the seller is saying and doing. But—whether intentionally or not—this is misdirecting.

You can think of this another way: Every business is a theater production. There's a front stage and a backstage. When people see a stage production, they're focused on what's happening on the front stage. It sucks up all of the oxygen, and it gets the most attention. When there's a bad stage production, everyone will say, "What bad acting! What bad dancing! If only they'd cast someone else!" Am I saying the actor doesn't make a difference? No. Actors matter. But when you put a good actor in front of a bad backstage, that actor's not going to have the supporting structure to unlock the full potential of their performance.

It's the backstage, the plumbing, the logistics, the little things that no one talks about, that make up the difference between winners and the rest. That underlying element is revenue operations. In other words, revenue operations is the logistics of your revenue engine.

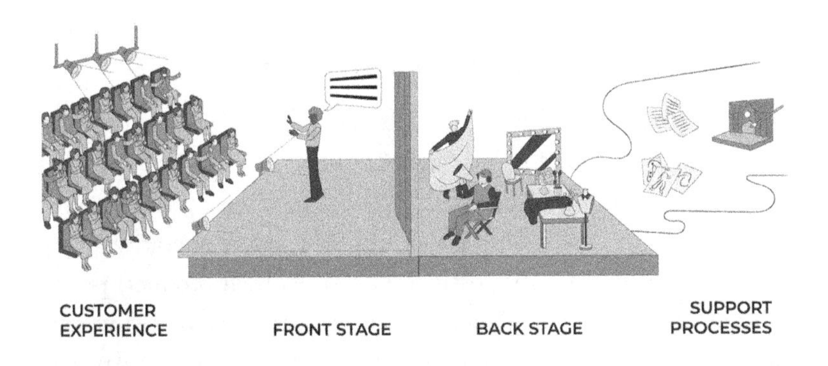

Companies have invested more money than ever in their tech stacks. Their databases are larger than they've ever been. Despite a decade of ongoing predictions that the number of salespeople is going to decrease, there are more salespeople than ever before. Companies are building Ferrari exteriors with hamster wheel engines. Then, they're pouring high-octane fuel in and wondering, "Why isn't this working?" Despite all of these big shows of spending and investments for great efficiency, companies have to work harder and spend more to capture less and less. If you look at any financial metric over time in the business world, you see degradation. You see diminishing returns. And the only way that those companies can counteract degradation is volume, volume, volume.

Even as I write this book, we are seeing an inevitable fraying in corporate America. Trust levels are at their lowest. We're in the midst of what is being called "the Great Resignation." Why is it happening? Because the underlying plumbing is made of quarter-inch copper and foil. So many companies in every industry have not built the plumbing to support what they're doing, and that's led to the unsustainability and turbulence so many people are experiencing in every facet of their lives today.

So...what is revenue operations?

Revenue operations is managing the ambiguities, the conflicts, and the gaps that exist within the processes and methodologies for how companies execute their business model, successfully deliver their value proposition, win and retain customers, and generate revenue.

WHAT IS *NOT* REVENUE OPERATIONS?

One of the trends that I've seen over the last couple of years as the topic of RevOps has become increasingly popular is that its meaning has become increasingly ambiguous.

Because of the increasing popularity of revenue operations (and because they want to justify their roles and sell their product) people and companies have kind of hooked whatever they do onto revenue operations. I have seen people refer to revenue operations as nearly every facet of a business. But for it to reach its true full impact, it's just as important to understand what RevOps *isn't* as it is to understand what RevOps is.

For example, revenue operations is not corporate strategy. Revenue operations is not customer acquisition. It's not sales. It's not demand generation. It's not the marketing function. When people say things like, "Who's responsible for company growth?" Revenue operations has a role in that, but it isn't itself what revenue operations is.

THE CRUCIAL ROLE OF STRATEGIC REVENUE OPERATIONS

Brian Halligan, the former CEO and current Executive Chairman of HubSpot, said at the 2017 Inbound event, "It's never been easier to start a company. But it's never been harder to scale."

Consider how rare it used to be for someone to have a blog, send an email, or post a video online. Now, everybody can do these things with the press of a button. Technology hasn't only become better, but cheaper; kids are walking around with supercomputers in their pockets. With the advent of better, cheaper tech comes a busier, noisier market. The quantity and quality of competition is greater than ever before. When the barriers to entry are so much lower and it's so much easier to do things, the small differences at the higher end begin to matter more and more. It's not possible to overstate how disproportionate the distribution of success is in today's market. It's easier than ever to start a business but astronomically harder to succeed. Good isn't good enough anymore.

Good ideas have less impact than ever before, and one flash in the pan is not going to grow a business. Every company that has gotten to a certain point, let's say a million dollars of revenue, is a company that's good at something. They might even occasionally be great at something. But why does "good" not always translate into outcomes? This is where consistency mastery matters; and the backend, almost invisible, discipline of strategic RevOps matters. In baseball, they give you a round ball and a round bat and tell you your job is to hit the ball squarely. One home run is a fluke; one hundred home runs is a reflection of consistency of skill. In business, the ability to understand and execute upon a framework with consistency will differentiate between a quick failure and continued success.

The crucial purpose of strategic revenue operations is maintaining that consistency.

I wouldn't be the first person to recognize the value of consistency. There's tons of research and firsthand accounts on how consistency of performance leads to greatness. The question is: How do you bring consistency into the world we are currently in? We are operating in complex dynamic systems, and that changes the entire game.

Many years ago, management consultant and author Peter Drucker said, "Businesses rarely go out of business because of starvation. Indigestion is far more likely the cause."

Plenty of people will think that the greatest threat to a business is a lack of opportunity. But the real threat is the inability to absorb and sustain the opportunities that they do have. In other words, complexity is the toxin of growth. Many companies focus on increasing force, as if they could battle their way through complexity using sheer numbers alone. Sales and marketing have always been the focus. More sales, more marketing! That leads to more growth!

...but once you hit a certain level of force, applying more force will only give diminishing returns. Managing complexity, however, is highly leverageable. That's why strategic revenue operations plays a crucial role in achieving more for less. It's all about managing complexity to unlock greater returns from the force that is already being applied.

Entropy is always increasing; that's the second law of thermodynamics. In terms of a natural organizational dynamic, that entropy is disorder and randomness. In business, disorder means complexity. As a business grows, or even sustains, complexity is always increasing. That's not a bug; it's a feature. So you can't "fix" it or skip it; you have to manage it.

That entropy, that complexity, is what we often call friction. The challenging thing to accept is that friction is a part of growth. You cannot eliminate friction, nor should you. Friction is a force that is neither good nor bad. It simply is a factor of business. It shouldn't be ignored, and it frankly can't be avoided when it comes to scaling or sustaining growth.

THE SEVEN DISCIPLINES OF STRATEGIC REVOPS

The job of revenue operations is to solve as much of the problem and eliminate as much of the negative friction and complexity as possible before it gets to execution. Strategic revenue operations does all of this through the focus on seven disciplines, which can be further sorted into two groups. The first four disciplines of RevOps concentrate on the day-to-day, week-to-week focus of revenue operations. You might call them the tactical components of revenue operations. The last three disciplines are strategic components. Taken together, these seven areas lead strategic revenue operations to build the genius into the system. This is what enables revenue growth. This is what generates lift.

1. DATABASE MANAGEMENT

Data is crucial. Today, the database is far more than a storage bin of contact information and a history of activities. In a well-aligned, high-performing organization, the database is the core; it fuels everything. If you don't have a robust database, you'll be paying a significant friction tax. The complexity associated with managing databases is the primary reason why there's a need for strategic revenue operations.

Some of the critical areas of responsibility in database management are:

- Managing and maintaining the database
- Ensuring data integrity
- Managing segmentation
- Unifying data across functions in departments
- Establishing and managing a data management service level agreement

2. PROCESS COMPLIANCE AND OPTIMIZATION

What are the processes used to manage the customer/user experience? How are you ensuring the utilization of those systems and being in accordance with those processes? These are the systems that enable our teams to work in the day-to-day, minute-to-minute, and execute in a low-friction environment. Without effective management, those areas are fraught with small conflicts that lead to significant friction and overwhelming complexity. Revenue operations ensures that processes are being followed and that the systems, tools, and processes are being used as intended.

The challenge of this second discipline is understanding the origins of process compliance and optimization. It doesn't come from dogma. People will sometimes hear "compliance" and mistakenly think, "Oh, this is how we'll do it because it is what it is. We must comply with the status quo." That's not the compliance I'm talking about. I'm talking about the situations where people fall out of compliance with the process, when salespeople stop following the methodology, when the CRM isn't updated. Understanding the *failure of compliance* is crucial to optimization. So it's not compliance in the combative or dictatorial sense. It's compliance in the learning and iterative sense. The world and systems we operate in are always changing. If the change outside the organization exceeds the change of its internal processes, then the organization creates its own friction, complexity, and problems.

3. DESIGN, ALIGN, MANAGE, AND OPTIMIZE THE TECH STACK

More money than ever before is being spent on technology. Yet, technology rarely delivers the outcomes that justify the price tag. According to data from Forrester Research, which was published in May 2020 under "Effective Sales Operations: Are We There Yet?", CRMs fail to deliver on their expected impact at a 50 to nearly 70 percent level. Maintenance is a big part of management and optimization of tech, so effective strategic revenue operations needs to:

- Define the core requirements for all revenue-focused applications
- Manage the backend and technical aspects of the core and primary segments of the tech stack
- Ensure applications solve for the organization (not just for specific instances)
- Regularly prune and update and align the tech stack

4. TERRITORY AND COMPENSATION MANAGEMENT

The overall structure and approach for the organization should be determined by your company's senior team, the team that is responsible for setting the strategy. Within those constraints, revenue operations is responsible for identifying:

- How territories get broken up

- What the underlying focus should be
- How we are segmenting, aligning, and ensuring that we meet the underlying economic model associated with our go-to-market strategy

5. DATA SCIENCE, ANALYTICS, AND METRICS

My company, which is relatively small, creates more new data in a day than a human can meaningfully consume in a lifetime. In the early 1990s, I remember doing seminars about the importance of data and metrics. At these events, my mom (yes, it was a family-owned business) would say, "We're drowning in data, yet starved for knowledge." I wonder how she would describe the circumstances today.

Getting the right data in the right way at the right time and ensuring that the right people receive it (and in the best manner possible to utilize it!) is increasingly a competitive advantage. Within the next 24 months, effective use of data won't just be an advantage; it'll be a ticket to the ballpark. What's involved in data science, analytics, and metrics?

- Setting up the data gathering process
- Building out and managing appropriate dashboards
- Curating and driving the insights to the relevant people who stimulate new tests and inform existing ones

6. PREDICTABILITY

One of the key components of a successful revenue operations team is building predictability into people. Forecasting and ongoing assessments and adjustments are an inevitable part of structuring your business's strategic revenue operations and framework. Structure is everything. Structure is the invisible force. It's what Adam Smith, author of *The Wealth of Nations*, called the "invisible hand."

The structure is the underlying system design. Your system is perfectly designed to produce the experiences you have right now. So, if you want to change the experience, you have to change the underlying system. Here, we're talking about complex systems that are all interacting with each other. So it encompasses the underlying system design, the tools, the tech, and the scoreboard. All of this builds upon structure, which leads to greater predictability.

If you want to know how important that structure and scoreboard are, all you have to do is compare how a bunch of 12-year-old kids play any game before and after someone says, "Hey guys! Let's keep score!"

What changes when people keep score? Well, the intensity of effort changes, and whatever is being scored becomes the new objective. Years ago, when I was coaching my son's soccer team, the kids used to play what I'd call amoeba soccer. It was a blob of kids following the ball. To fix this problem, I simply changed the scoring mechanism. Instead of scoring the goals, I scored how many times the team passed the ball before they took a shot. This incentivized the kids to play differently, to strategize, and to actually position themselves across the field to improve their pass rate. I changed the underlying system to achieve a greater outcome.

Whether it's a kids' soccer team or the performance of a sales team, predictability is a major strategic element that is affected by the structure and design of the system. Why do salespeople have such a bad rep? Well, their score is commissions. It's not that sales can only be motivated by commission, but that's what most companies track on the scoreboard. And whatever is being scored becomes something people will pay attention to and pursue. Part of strategic revenue operations is iterating and managing the structure of the system—the design, tools, tech, and scoreboard—in order to guide performance, behavior, and predictability.

7. BEHAVIORAL SCIENCE AND USER EXPERIENCE

A great way to understand the difference in design and user experience is to think of how people cross a parking lot. You've got the paved walkway that wraps around the lot and then the trampled grass that makes a beeline toward the parking spots. The pavement is design. The dirt path is the user experience. Why do people do what they do? This question applies both internally and externally. Why do our people do the things that they do? Why do our customers do things the way they do?

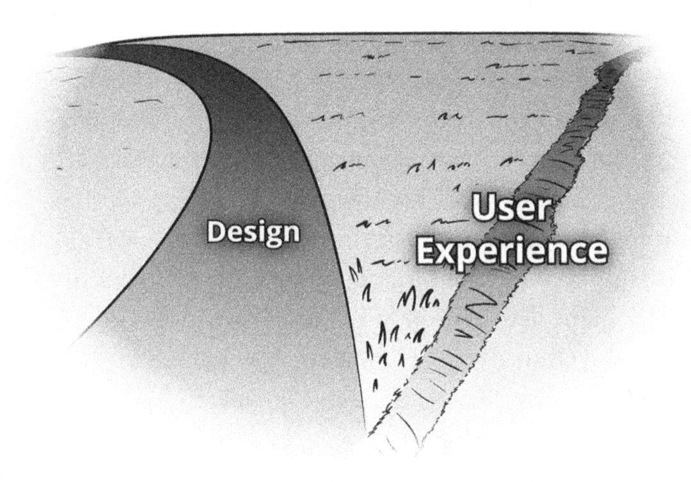

One of the dangers of modern sales and marketing in my experience is that we are auto-tuning our businesses, our salespeople, and our go-to-market efforts. We tend to design our processes and laboratories without knowing how they will really work, and we're turning human nature into the bug rather than the feature.

When we are confronted with the human element, and because humans are inherently less predictable, we are inclined to treat it as a bug. And when companies are focused on efficiency rather than efficacy, speed rather than velocity, then everything unpredictable or inefficient can look like a bug. Efficiency is all about eliminating variants, but that tactic ignores the fact that there is good variance and bad variance.

If you look at variance from a more positive perspective, every business is in mass pursuit of great differentiation and distinction from competitors, right? An underlying principle of business is to differentiate or die. Difference is a form of positive friction. It's high-value friction. But difference is not efficient, so many organizations think it must be squashed.

As speed and efficiency-oriented technology has taken hold, we've seen how the increased capacity and volume of email has led to an inevitable efficiency of sending thousands of crappy, shitty emails, just like everyone else. We're over-designing and over-processing. Through this fixation on efficiency and eliminating variants, we're turning salespeople into bots.

The thing is that sales and marketing is all about the communication and influence of human behavior, yet very few people in these spaces actually embrace behavioral economics or behavioral science. The implementation of behavioral science is treated like cheap parlor tricks, and the nuanced role of human nature is trivialized as a bug of an efficient system. This kind of adversarial thinking leads to bad elements and blindspots in the development of strategic revenue operations.

At the end of the day, part of revenue operations is applying behavioral models and optimizing the user experience. Successful internal management and leadership are about influencing behavior, the actions we take, and the decisions we make. If you want to influence an effective, positive outcome, you must pay attention to and account for how humans actually behave, not how you think they should behave.

THE GREATER GOAL

After sharing the seven disciplines of revenue operations, I want to make one thing absolutely clear: The goal of revenue operations is not to optimize revenue operations.

Each element of revenue operations has its own independent pieces. Improving any one area will lead to improvements for the overarching organization. When you actually work these elements together, holistically, you are optimizing the organization. You are optimizing the experience. It's easy to get lost in the process with all of these intertwining, complex moving parts, but remember that the real objective of strategic revenue operations is to solve for the customer and achieve revenue objectives with the least effort possible.

CONSIDERATION BEFORE COMMITMENT

Before committing to your revenue operations, you have to consider which of the two main elements of revenue operations you're looking at. There's the tactical element, and there's the strategic element.

Tactical revenue operations will improve the organization, though it will be incremental improvement. You will likely not attribute any major change in the organization to tactical revenue operations. However, it is still an important part of the operations as a whole. In fact, you've probably already been doing tactical revenue operations without realizing it. But the unconscious choice to do revenue operations is not really a choice at all. If you want revenue operations to be a driver of growth and performance, then you must be aware of the choice you are making, and you have to understand what that choice means for your organization. It's so easy for people to pick up the buzzword "revenue operations." But if all I'm doing is pointing at things and calling them revenue operations, then I'm not fundamentally changing the underlying elements that produce results. This means I'm not going to be able to change the results.

Strategic revenue operations is the ultimate strategic decision, and it is a conscious one. It's far more than putting an admin on function-coordinating activities or bringing a group of people together. It requires a strong strategy.

From the book, *Good Strategy, Bad Strategy* by Richard Rumelt, a strong strategy has three elements. First, a strong diagnosis that clearly defines the challenge. Second, a guiding policy which, like the guard rails on a highway, directs and constrains action in certain directions without defining exactly what shall be done. Third, a set of coherent actions that dictate how the guiding policy will be carried out.

There should be constructive tension between revenue operations and the disciplines that it is optimizing and aligning. Sales, marketing, and success are focused on the force side, while revenue operations is managing the side of consistency and friction. It's the two sides coming together that creates velocity for your business.

For revenue operations to be at its most effective, it cannot be subordinate to the sales, marketing, or success functions. Those other three functions worship at the altar of force. They are inherently force-focused disciplines, so they will always trade off to increase force. When you put revenue operations under one of the force disciplines, then it will always trade off to that discipline, and you'll lose the strategic contributions inherent in strategic revenue operations.

Successful strategy is about managing trade-offs. This is also a major reason why revenue operations doesn't need to be subordinate to another discipline, because complexity and bad friction will already be eliminated through the successful management of trade-offs. Revenue operations should have clearly defined jobs so that decisions surrounding those trade-offs can be made and managed effectively.

When you are considering the efficacy of your revenue operations, remember that its role is to manage consistency and mitigate complexity. There is no singular "right way" to revenue operations. It's not about fixing. It's about managing trade-offs.

COMMON MISTAKES

The biggest mistake people make is implementing revenue operations without having the organizational commitment to the operations' purpose. Without that commitment, revenue operations becomes just another department. It creates bad friction and needless complexity. Revenue operations, improperly managed, becomes the department of sales prevention.

Because revenue operations addresses the invisible, there needs to be a commitment to letting it be invisible and solve the invisible. When there's a lack of organizational understanding, you will end up with a mismanaged revenue operations that gets pushed into a support role beneath sales, marketing, and success. It ends up creating more conflict than it solves.

People will also make the common mistake of falling into operations. In other words, people mistakenly think that operations is the keyword of revenue operations. It's really easy to fall into the cyclical pattern of optimizing the process and implementing the process for the sake of optimizing and implementing the process. It's almost instinctive to jump from managing friction to eliminating friction. We may become obsessed, almost maniacal, about eliminating friction in an effort to optimize things to run faster, faster, faster. But wait. That is mistaking speed for velocity.

Do not forget to use friction to your benefit. Remember that friction is a tool; it is neither inherently good nor bad. The goal of revenue operations is not to eliminate all friction. The goal is to eliminate friction where it is of low value and add it where it has higher value. This is how we get from point A to point B with the least amount of disruption, by prioritizing our velocity over our speed.

One final pitfall to remain vigilant of is developing a champagne taste on a beer budget. In other words, try not to have eyes that are bigger than your stomach. It's easy to get swept up in the hype of a new buzzword and start talking about revenue operations in the context of these grand, impractical schemes. Excitedly, you might start hyping up these big plans, how everything is going to be made easier, and every salesperson's job is going to become this and that. But your organization might not have the tolerance or resources to handle all that change.

It is important that your revenue operations is a tangible, realistic component incorporated in your organizational strategy, not an aspiration that's orbiting on the outside, out of reach.

TIPS AND TAKEAWAYS

In Chapter 2, we covered the fundamental need for revenue operations and the seven major disciplines of strategic RevOps. When implementing effective revenue operations into your business, it is important to:

- Remember that the keyword of RevOps is not "operations" but "revenue,"
- Treat revenue operations as equal to, not subordinate to, the force disciplines of sales, marketing, and customer success,
- Set realistic objectives for your revenue operations,
- Use revenue operations to optimize your business, not the operations itself,
- And accept the inevitability of friction and use it as a tool to manage complexity.

The difference between winners and losers, of big brands and their mid-market competitors, is neither merit, nor skill, nor the quality of their ideas. It is a difference of strategy. The crucial role of strategic revenue operations is in structuring and managing the trade-offs that lead to more effective outcomes. And while there is no singular "correct" path to success, there is the Revenue Acceleration Framework, which we will discuss in greater depth in Part II of this book.

With the additional strategies found within the Framework, you will be able to further optimize your business' revenue and growth objectives and start gaining more juice for the squeeze.

CHAPTER 3

WHY FRAMEWORKS ARE IMPORTANT

I USED TO PARTICIPATE IN A CEO PEER GROUP WHERE WE MET every month and talked about various things, and I found myself getting bored and frustrated with how often some people would use "strategy" as a buzzword in conversations. This is a strategy, those are strategies. We're strategizing over here, we're being strategic over there. But what is "strategic" about using a buzzword without demonstrating any underlying understanding of its meaning? What is strategy?

I was curious to see how many different things "strategy" could mean to people having the same conversation. So during one of those monthly peer group meetings, when I found myself talking with a group of 12 CEOs, I started tracking how many times the word "strategy" was used. Over the course of a 35-minute conversation, my little tick chart was used 42 times—42 instances of "strategy," averaging more than one "strategy" per minute. I also kept a loose count of how many times the word "strategy" was used with entirely different contexts and meanings; there were about 40 changes in the definition of the word. For over half an hour, more than once per minute, one of the 12 CEOs had talked "strategy" to the rest of us while also meaning something entirely different than the previous CEO who'd talked "strategy."

Strategy is one of those words that everyone knows, and it's also one of those words that make us feel smart when we use it. It allows you to assume that everyone understands the same thing because everyone just sprinkled a generous amount of "strategy" into the conversation. When there's no attempt to align our perspectives, we all walk away saying, "Yes, everyone thinks strategy is important." And that's it. No greater conclusion can be drawn from that kind of conversation other than the fact that people agreed on the importance of some words. Then everyone splits off to pursue whatever their definition of "strategy" is based on their limited perceptions.

If you're lucky enough, someone will eventually say, "Hang on...I thought we were going with [strategy A]."

And finally, the next person might realize, "Oh, when you said strategy, you meant [strategy A]? Well, I was just trying to execute [strategy B] like everybody else."

Which is when everybody else would chime in with, "Woah, I thought when you said strategy, you meant [strategy C/D/E/F/G]! Because that's what strategy is really all about."

And if you're extra lucky, your organization can then regroup and realign things correctly against a framework. But if your business, like most, has an average amount of luck and you don't notice when this misalignment occurs, everybody will keep operating in opposite directions until things fall apart.

The inevitable decline of a misaligned organization proves the importance of having a conscious perspective. Does your "strategy" have to be the exact same as the next guy's "strategy" all the time? Not necessarily, in the same way that not everyone has to be defining and perceiving every action and every waypoint of the organization's growth journey the exact same way. But there must be an understanding and acceptance of how diversity of perspectives can create misalignment, which must then be managed.

ALIGNING VECTORS

You've probably already heard this parable: A group of blind men heard that a strange animal, called an elephant, had been brought to the town, but none of them were aware of its shape and form. Out of curiosity, they said, "We must inspect and know it by touch, of which we are capable." So they sought it out, and when they found it they groped about it. The first person, whose hand landed on the trunk, said, "This being is like a thick snake." For another one whose hand reached its ear, it seemed like a kind of fan. Yet another person, whose hand was upon its leg, said, "This elephant is a pillar, like a tree trunk." The blind man who placed his hand upon its side described the elephant as a big wall. Another who felt its tail described it as a rope. The last blind man, feeling the elephant's tusk, stated the elephant is that which is hard, smooth, and like a spear.

In business, sales and marketing is your elephant. All too often, sales, marketing, and customer success organizations are misaligned; different people are seeing different things and basing their own decisions off of their own perspectives. And even when you think you're doing it right, just like everybody else, you're actually optimizing for the individual discipline. You get better and better at what you do, but it never translates into actual growth.

When Dharmesh Shah, the co-founder and CTO of HubSpot, asked Elon Musk, "What's the most important thing you would do to successfully grow a business?" Elon's response was simply, "Align your vectors."

But how exactly do we "align our vectors"? We can start by defining those vectors.

Vectors are all of the inputs that cause outcomes to happen. The challenge, then, is ensuring that all of these vectors are aligned when there are way more inputs within one organization than we can even imagine. If you were to aim for a pure alignment, you'd need to put yourself in an echo chamber. When an organization is purely and perfectly aligned, there is only a single form of thought that everyone would agree with. But that's not how organizations and businesses realistically operate. With additional people and additional inputs, diversity increases and alignment decreases. Alignment and diversity have an inverse relationship. Therefore, growing a business is an ongoing act of maintaining stability in an unstable environment. You need to align different perspectives, different viewpoints, and different experiences so the whole is greater than the sum of its parts.

The problem is that diversity also involves unspoken experiences (invisible stimuli, if you will) which have as much impact on how somebody does what they do or how they interpret things as any visible experiences. And nowhere is this invisible stimuli more prevalent than in the world of sales and marketing, where even the most common words mean completely different things to different people.

Take a look at any popular marketing methodology today. There's inbound marketing, account-based marketing, outbound marketing, and so on. What do they all mean? It depends on who you ask, right? People might think they're communicating clearly with each other, and it looks like there's alignment around these terms. It sounds like everyone is saying the same thing. But in reality, everyone is hearing and interpreting things very differently based on their own perspective.

ALIGNING TO A FRAMEWORK

This all gets into why I love frameworks. Frameworks give us something to align ourselves against so we all know we're operating at the same velocity and the business as a whole is headed in the right direction. Frameworks take the inherent meanings out of words and turn them into a picture. In other words, frameworks represent the whole.

The problem with words is that words are absorbed linearly. If the words in a sentence are out of order, you have a tough time deriving the intended meaning of those words. Or, the meaning may change entirely because of that dependence on linear understanding. But a picture, a framework, is different. It presents the whole as one. Succeeding in a complex discipline like go-to-market requires deep understanding and execution of very specific disciplines. You wouldn't want to miss the forest for the trees; you certainly wouldn't want to miss the whole for the parts when it comes to marketing and growth strategies.

However, companies will often attempt to align themselves around their journey, rather than their destination. This puts a drag on revenue growth, especially as a company's opportunities and other vectors increase. They make the mistake of fixating on technical details in how they get to the waypoints of the journey, rather than the destination. When companies are instead able to see the bigger picture—the framework—of their growth operations, they are able to free up the paths for people and vectors to take their best course of action toward the destination.

This is ultimately my intention behind creating the Revenue Acceleration Framework, to provide the picture that we've spent years studying and looking for and digging into. The Framework is the whole which reflects my understanding of the underlying difference between companies that put forth the effort and get massive gains and successes and the companies that put forth an equivalent effort with equivalent product strategies, but don't see those massive successes. The Framework was created to highlight those differences and answer some key questions about the growth and revenue strategies of businesses.

What are the best companies doing that others might not be doing? More importantly, what are they *not* doing that others might be doing? One of the biggest surprises for me when researching the Revenue Acceleration Framework was that the super-successful companies tended to do less than the companies that were struggling. Intuitively, we're led to believe that effort equals results. You put more effort in, you gain more traction. When I initially formed the theory around the Framework, I thought that I was going to find the secret tactics that successful companies were doing that other companies weren't doing. But what I actually found were the many things that successful companies weren't doing which the other companies, for whatever reason, were. The successful companies were simplifying things and reducing complexity. They were focused on velocity whereas others were focused on speed. The successful companies were aiming to get more juice for the squeeze while everyone else was just squeezing harder and harder.

"JOBS TO BE DONE" THEORY

Another aspect that a lot of less-successful companies will mistakenly focus on is the process, rather than our objective. We get tied into what we're doing, and forget why we're doing it. We become fixated on the process and forget that the same action or feature in one situation can be a home run, while in another situation it can be the nail in the coffin of success.

One of my favorite questions is, "What's the problem we're trying to solve here?" In the world of strategy, this question can be answered with the "Jobs to Be Done" theory. This theory basically says that people don't actually buy things. What they're doing is hiring things.

There was this great study done by Clayton Christensen, author of *Competing with Luck*, about a major research project McDonald's funded to increase the sales of its milkshakes. Researchers repeatedly observed people buying milkshakes, and then interviewed them. Through the duration of the research, it was determined that people bought milkshakes at different times of the day. Some people bought 'em in the morning. Some people bought 'em in the afternoon. Some people bought 'em in the evening.

While in each case, the thing being bought was a milkshake, the job being done by the milkshake was different depending on the time of day. For example, in the morning, people who were buying milkshakes tended to be on their commute to work, and they were buying a milkshake as a breakfast replacement. They wanted something that would fill them up. Or (and personally, I found this really interesting) some people actually bought the milkshake as a sort of pleasurable distraction for what was to be an otherwise monotonous and uneventful work day. All of the morning milkshake-buyers were looking for a quick purchasing experience; order the shake, get the shake, and get on the road to work.

The job the milkshakes were being "hired" to do was very different in the afternoon. At that time of day, people were coming in with their families or they were maybe taking an afternoon break. Then, the milkshake was fulfilling a role of relaxation. People were still buying milkshakes, just like in the morning, but the entire rationale behind why they were buying that milkshake (therefore the experiences and factors that would lead to increasing sales for the milkshake) was very different. While

McDonald's may have been selling the exact same chocolate, vanilla, or strawberry shakes, people were "hiring" something very different depending on the underlying context and the job that was being done.

The way we should define jobs for products is the same way we would define jobs for people, or the same way we would define a new position if we were hiring an individual to be on our staff. In business, we tend to look at tactics. We tend to look at strategies. We tend to look at products through the lens of "buying" or "doing" when what we really should be thinking about is, "Why are we doing this?" and "What's the job being done here?" That's the important perspective shift central to the Jobs to Be Done theory.

TIPS AND TAKEAWAYS

In Chapter 3, we covered the importance of alignment, the Jobs to Be Done theory, and the four key components of the go-to-market approach. When using this knowledge to structure the go-to-market approach for your business, it is important to:

- Understand the inverse relationship between diversity and alignment,
- Align your vectors (the inputs that affect your outcomes) to your framework,
- And identify the Jobs to Be Done of both your products and your people.

Humans aren't just bad at understanding complex concepts; we're also bad at communicating them to each other. This is why misalignment can be so dangerous for a business, no matter its size. When we're focused only on our own perspective, we become misaligned, and things tend to fall apart when pulled in opposite directions.

Fortunately, the four key components of your go-to-market approach serve as the important first steps toward the Framework, and that Framework will create the guideposts your business needs to realign its vectors toward a future point of revenue growth.

PART II

FOUR KEY COMPONENTS OF THE GO-TO-MARKET APPROACH

CHAPTER 4

GO-TO-MARKET STRATEGY

IN 1971, INTEL HAD A MAJOR DECISION TO MAKE.

Founded by Gordon Moore in 1965, just six years prior, Intel achieved tremendous success in its early days as a leading manufacturer of memory chips for computers. But by the 1970s, the company faced even greater competition from manufacturers in Asia. The market was shifting and the lower-cost chips from its overseas competitors were threatening Intel's position as a leader in the industry, not to mention cutting into Intel's revenues, margins, and profits.

Andy Grove, who went on to become the CEO of Intel and the man largely credited for leading the company's transformation into the juggernaut that it is today, met with Moore to discuss what decisions Intel would make to adapt to the shifting market. As described by Grove in his book, *Only the Paranoid Survive*:

> I asked Moore, "If we got kicked out and the board brought in a new CEO, what do you think he would do?"
>
> Gordon answered without hesitation. "He would get us out of memories."

I stared at him, numb, then said, "Why shouldn't you and I walk out the door, come back, and do it ourselves?"

Big decisions aren't only made to combat competition, either. In 2006, HubSpot saw early success as a startup that provides a digital marketing platform for growing businesses. For years, their focus was split between two target markets, each represented by a distinct persona:

Owner Ali, **a small business owner** with less than ten employees and no full-time marketing experience.

Mary Marketer, **a marketing manager** who worked in a company with between ten and a thousand employees.

But as HubSpot moved to scale up, it faced barriers and had to make a big decision to adjust—not for the sake of its competitors, but for the sake of its customers.

To quote Brian Halligan, HubSpot's CEO at the time, "By trying to serve multiple personas, we were serving none of them. It was only when we decided that Mary Marketer was our sole target market that we began to rapidly grow the number of customers we acquired without the return falling apart."

Strategy is all about making choices, and both Intel and HubSpot demonstrated a crucial success factor in defining your go-to-market strategy.

THE FIVE QUESTIONS OF GO-TO-MARKET STRATEGY

The second element of an effective go-to-market approach is the strategy, and an effective go-to-market strategy should sufficiently answer the following five questions:

1. What is your business model and how can you best exploit it?
   A. If you want more information on defining and designing your business model, I encourage you to check out *Business Model Generation* by Alexander Osterwalder.
2. Who do you want to be a hero to?

    A. You get the answer to this question by providing a clear description of your ideal customer or ideal client profile, your target personas, and the Jobs to Be Done.
3. How does your value proposition stand out and resonate with your customers while distinguishing you from your competitive and alternative options?
    A. An important point to remember here is that your competition is made up of direct competitors, indirect competitors, alternative approaches, and the biggest competition of all—nothing. Everyone, including you, me, and the neighbors, can always choose to do nothing.
4. How will we position ourselves in our selected markets to achieve the right message fit that resonates with our target market to stimulate meaningful conversations?
5. How will we profitably acquire and retain customers and revenue?

Some people will see these five questions and think that only the correct strategy will address all five of these questions. That's not entirely true. Technically, every go-to strategy should answer these five fundamental questions, or it wouldn't be much of a strategy at all. But if not through the five questions, how else do we know if our strategy is the right one? Well, a strategy is not a single path, and there isn't one single strategy to success. A common myth of strategy is that it predetermines action. If you were to ask before implementing a strategy, "Is this the *right* strategy?" The answer is, it's not. You won't know if it's the "right" strategy until after the fact.

THE MOST IMPORTANT QUESTION YOU CAN ANSWER TO DRIVE YOUR GROWTH

Choosing who you want to do business with isn't natural for entrepreneurs, marketers, sales executives, or anyone for that matter. Because one way or another, we've all been conditioned with a degree of "scarcity" mentality. We're under constant pressure to hit our numbers, and we have a constant fear that we won't. As a result, we tend to define our market way too broadly for fear that if we leave anyone out, that might just be the reason that we fail.

The reality is that you can only be the best choice for a segment of your addressable market. The more time you spend trying to win over just anybody, the less distinct and the less special your business becomes.

When you define your market too broadly, when you define your customer base too broadly, you end up falling in the middle. And as we referenced earlier, good isn't good enough. You might be a little bit better than others, but there's not enough distinction for that to matter. Your customers don't have time to think about what makes you different from other options out there. So if you don't establish that distinction, you're going to fall into the "good enough" trench.

THE NECESSITY OF REVISION

What you should be aiming for is a good strategy. This brings us back to the three criteria of a good strategy established in Chapter 2: a diagnosis of the underlying issue, a guiding policy, and a set of coherent actions. In other words, we cannot aim for the right strategy because we don't have superpowers and can't see into the future. What we're aiming for is a good strategy because a good, effective strategy has a higher probability of creating a positive outcome and being the right strategy in retrospect.

Any strategy is "wrong" far, far more often than it's "right." This isn't just true for go-to-market strategies either. Consider the flight paths of commercial aircraft. Did you know planes are off course for the vast majority of their flight?

That statistic might seem strange to you if you've taken any flight and still ended up in the right place. So how does a plane fly off course nearly the entire flight and land at the correct airport? During the flight, pilots will make small tweaks constantly to keep the plane on course. So even though it is always minutely off course for the entire flight, the plane will still (hopefully) arrive at the designated destination.

I've also read somewhere that a bad strategy that's revised constantly is better than a good strategy that's never revised. But I would take it a step further and say, "There's no such thing as a good strategy that's never revised." If there is no tweaking and no course-correcting, it's not really a strategy. It's a dictate.

As long as the end point is defined and the freedom to make those minute adjustments is given to pilots and the people in your organization, everyone and everything will arrive at their designated destination.

TIPS AND TAKEAWAYS

In Chapter 4, we expanded upon the second element of the go-to-market approach: the economic strategy. When you are constructing that strategy for your business, it is important to:

- Be able to answer the five questions of an effective go-to-market strategy,
- Aim for a good strategy, not the "right" strategy,
- And define your endpoint and course-correct when necessary.

There are no strategies that predetermine success in the market, only strategies that "worked" or "did not work" in retrospect. However, don't let this sense of uncertainty convince you that strategy is unimportant when it comes to an effective go-to-market approach.

Seen another way, a good strategy is all about change and the freedom of choice. If you are willing to ask yourself the right questions and adjust the course of your strategy, you will be able to fulfill the second component of your approach successfully.

CHAPTER 5

THE ECONOMIC MODEL

AS ONE OF THE GREAT PHILOSOPHERS, FORREST GUMP, ONCE SAID, "Shit happens."

In complex systems and complex environments, we don't know all the factors that will influence the outcomes of the system we operate in. Sales and marketing is a unique discipline in business because it's an open-loop system, meaning you only control a portion of the system, the market controls most of it. In such a market, you don't get to where you want to by going in a straight line. So, you'd better know the "centerpoint" and the key contributors to getting there.

THE IMPORTANCE OF A GO-TO-MARKET APPROACH

In today's world, rich with innovation in every aspect of every market, we don't know what the specifics of the market environment will be like even just six months into the future. This is why the go-to-market approach exists to be a guiding policy. Your approach is defined by clear choices, and it provides those guardrails that we can use to remain actionable during very turbulent and disruptive times.

All of the perspective shifts we discussed in Chapter 3 around the

Jobs to Be Done and the realignment of vectors contributes to a strong go-to-market approach. Your go-to-market approach is the start of your business' revenue acceleration. It's a job that goes beyond sales, marketing, and customer success. Without a clear go-to-market approach, you can't actually have alignment that leads to revenue acceleration. Without defining your go-to-market approach, you can't increase your velocity. You can't align your vectors because there's nothing to align towards.

Fundamentally, the go-to-market approach is about making clear choices. Those choices are going to drive the most important, most frequent invisible activity performed by every person in your organization.

Far too often, we want to be right; we're afraid of being wrong. We're trying to figure out what's the right thing to do. However, while there are certainly many wrong choices to be made, there are rarely any choices we can say, with a hundred percent certainty, are the right choice to make. If anything, there are just very bad choices and progressively less bad choices. Rather than focusing on being right all the time, which is impossible, it is far more effective to focus on making progressively better choices. "Being right" is purely circumstantial, so making choices should never be about being right. Making choices should be about managing trade-offs.

The trade-off decision happens when we choose where the line is drawn between those advantages and disadvantages. When you fail to make that choice, when you fail to make your trade-off decisions, you are left to the whims of your environment. Without a go-to-market approach built on clear and defined choices, you are unable to control the set of your sales and are therefore unable to control your own destiny. All of this leads us to the four key components of the go-to-market approach—the economic model, the go-to-market strategy, the sales model, and the messaging, positioning, and narrative.

The first of those components is the economic model, aka the numbers game.

THE UNAVOIDABLE GAME

They say business and sales is a numbers game.

And I have to say, as someone with more than three decades of experience working with growth-focused businesses, it frustrates me to no end to see how few people actually understand the numbers involved in their game. Despite the prevalence of the idea that business and sales is a numbers game, how many companies are using their numbers to define and assess their overall strategy toward their objectives?

The answer is, "Not enough."

So in this chapter, I'm going in-depth to explain the numbers you must understand to transform and scale growth. These are the numbers you must understand to align everybody in your organization toward the game you're trying to win and the outcomes you are trying to achieve. These are the numbers you must understand when you identify your economic model, the first key component of your go-to-market approach.

> Warning: The remainder of this section involves math.

DEFINING A CLEAR PERSPECTIVE

What is your underlying economic model? This is the first question you need to be able to answer. To do that, you must understand your numbers.

An effective economic model focuses on the important contributors and constraints that increase the predictability and success of your efforts.

In other words, how does your company transform revenue into profit and enterprise value? What's the math behind that revenue, and how does that math dictate how well you are doing and what you can do? The economic model involves quite a bit of math, and there's no way around it, unfortunately. This may also be the reason why the economic model doesn't get the attention that it deserves within many businesses' go-to-market approach; most people don't like math.

However, the failure to understand your economic model makes you the equivalent of Alice in Wonderland. When she asks the owl, "How do I get there?" And the owl asks, "Where are you going?" If your response to that question, like Alice, is simply, "I don't know," then, as the owl says, "Anywhere will get you there!"

When we recognize the importance of having a clear point of perspective, we must also recognize the vital role played by the economic model to create that clarity. You must be able to assess the decisions that you're making to manage the trade-offs that are a part of executing your go-to-market approach. Without a clear economic model, you can't make consistent decisions and judge them and improve; it is really the mathematical underpinning of your business.

TERMS TO DEFINE

There are a few main components to the economic model: lifetime value, acquisition, and the demand generation model, as well as a handful of other terms.

Anyone who's taken an MBA-level class on the economics of business would know that this chapter doesn't cover the entirety of it. By no means am I suggesting that what I'm sharing in this book is a fully comprehensive explanation of the economic model. What I'm focusing on are the key elements of the economic model necessary for small to mid-market companies who are seeking growth. Like much of the information in this book, it's about application, not theory.

ACV/ASV

The first number that I want to define for you is referred to typically as ACV or ASV. This number is the "all commodity value" or "average sales value." On average, how much revenue does a customer generate in a year? If you were to add up all the things that an average customer bought in a year, what would that equal? ACV is basically your total revenue within a time frame (usually one year) divided by the number of customers that created that revenue.

GROSS PROFIT, GROSS MARGIN

The next step in understanding the economic model is calculating your gross margin or gross profit. Gross profit is a dollar number, and gross margin is communicated as a percentage.

Gross profit is = **Revenue – Direct variable cost** of generating that revenue

In other words, gross profit is the incremental cost of making another sale. You'll see this number sometimes referred to as "cost of goods sold" or "sales revenue." (To note: every company will account for these things differently.)

Your gross margin is the percentage of what's left after subtracting the incremental cost of making a sale. Gross profit is the dollar value difference. As an example, say I've got a $1,000 sale price, and it costs me $200 to make that incremental sale. My gross margin would be 80 percent, and my gross profit would be $800.

If it costs $800 to make a $1,000 sale, then the gross margin would be 20 percent, and the gross profit would be $200.

LIFETIME VALUE

While I firmly believe you should look at your customers as the individual people and entities that they are...from an economic perspective, what you're acquiring is an asset. For the sake of your business's growth, you're making an investment. You're investing in your sales, marketing, and customer success efforts to acquire a revenue-producing asset. In many, many ways, it's the same underlying principle when you consider making an investment into a stock or a bond. In essence, lifetime value is the question of:

How many times will a customer buy from you?

Because we're using the average annual number in our first calculation, in this case we'll refer to the lifetime value as how many years a customer will buy from you on average.

If a customer generates $20,000 on average and your gross margin is

50 percent, you generate $10,000 of gross profit. If, on average, customers buy from you for five years, then the value of that customer is $50,000, calculated as **$10,000 gross profit × five years lifetime.**

CHURN

Churn is the percentage of customers that you lose per year. So, if you're in a recurring-revenue business (like a subscription service), then you would need to track churn.

As an example, if every year ten out of a hundred customers don't renew their annual subscription with me, my churn would be 10 percent.

From another perspective, you can also say that, with a churn of 10 percent, the average lifetime of your customers as revenue-generating assets is ten years.

REPEAT PURCHASE RATE

Repeat purchase rate is a term that we use when we have more of a transaction business or programmatic sale.

Let's say that you're in the office supplies business, and you sign a three-year contract. Or, you might not even have an established contract, but you're selling office supplies to companies who are in the habit of buying from you. There's no set rate that they're paying every year. So, there is no churn element based on an established subscription system.

But consider this: **What percentage of your customers will repeat their average purchase pattern from you every year?** That percentage would be your repeat purchase rate.

You might have read that question and thought, "Well, hang on. Aren't 'churn' and 'repeat purchase rate' kinda the same thing?"

Yes, but no. One could argue that churn and repeat purchase rate are basically calculating the same thing. However, **churn measures loss** and **repeat purchase rate measures retention**.

If I have a 33 percent churn rate, then my average lifetime is going to be 3 years.

ACQUISITION

The next calculation of the economic model to consider is what we call acquisition cost.

There are a lot of different ways to break down acquisition cost, but the easiest way to understand it is to answer the question: **How much money do you spend to acquire a customer?**

Lifetime Value Analysis

Average Sale Value	$ 27,500
Gross Margin	82%
Gross Profit	$ 22,550
Average Lifetime	7
Total Lifetime Value	$ 157,850
Year 1 Target Customers	39
Year 2 Target Customers	78
Year 3 Target Customers	118
Year 1 LTV	$ 6,156,150
Year 2 LTV	$ 12,312,300
Year 3 LTV	$ 18,626,300
Total LTV	$ 37,094,750

CAC Analysis

%LTV to CAC	25%
Target CAC	$ 39,462.50
New Customer Target	235
CAC Investment	$ 9,273,687.50

Acquisition cost can be the sum of a lot of things. It can include the salaries and commissions I pay my salespeople, the money that I'm spending with my marketing team, the cost of my advertising, the cost of the technology that I'm using for the marketing and advertising... All those expenses are directly related to the acquisition of new customers.

Except when it's not. An important thing to remember about acquisition costs is that, as is the case with most businesses, there are people and technology and tools responsible for both acquiring new customers and managing existing ones—in which case, you should not allocate 100 percent of your calculated costs to acquisition, as a part of those costs isn't oriented to acquisition. If a salesperson gets roughly two-thirds of their compensation for managing existing business and a third of their compensation for generating new business, then you should count only the third of what you're paying that salesperson toward your acquisition cost. The same applies to the cost of marketing, technology, etc.

With the acquisition cost, there's kind of a two by two here that you should keep in mind:

First, remember that what you're doing is making an investment in an asset that's going to produce revenue for a certain number of years. You should consider your acquisition cost from the standpoint of how much money you are comfortable spending to acquire a new customer.

Second, you should have a target in mind for the percentage of lifetime value that your acquisition represents. You should also track what the real lifetime value is once you've acquired your new customer.

The biggest barrier to growth acceleration that I see in companies, especially those that are not funded by outside sources, is that they're not actually investing enough money into customer acquisition. In the end, they never fully unlock their potential because they're only working with conservative spending estimates instead of calculating their actual acquisition costs so they can identify potential avenues for growth within their economic model.

There's a tendency for everyone to focus on the idea of efficiency, which means everyone wants to lower the number, lower the number, lower the number. A smaller cost is a better cost. But that is not always true. When you reach a certain point in developing your economic model, you should target a range for your acquisition cost, rather than trying to push it down further.

What the best businesses do is establish a target range where they keep their cost below a certain percentage and *above* a certain percentage. If the cost rises above a certain percentage, it's showing that the company's economic model is ineffective. If the cost drops below a certain percentage, it means that the company is most likely missing opportunities to generate profit.

DEMAND GENERATION

The last major element of the economic model which we will discuss is the demand generation model.

The first thing you must do to understand your demand generation is define your lead. You can use whatever terms that you want, but from a general perspective, I recommend that you define four tiers of lead for your business. (And the lead could be a person or an account depending upon what type of business that you are.)

The first level is what I like to call a qualified lead. Basically, does this lead appear to fit your ideal client profile?

A *marketing*-qualified lead adds an additional element to the first level of lead, where you're determining if the lead meets whatever criteria you've established, and whether you're going to direct any time, money, and energy toward this lead.

Some qualified leads will become latent leads. These are leads that you have identified, that you aren't doing anything actively to attract or pursue. In the future, those latent leads may find your business and become something more, but you are not doing anything otherwise.

A sales-qualified (or marketing-qualified) lead meets the criteria and, from a sales or marketing perspective, there's a level of activity directed toward that lead. These leads are the opportunities you are pursuing.

Like every other element of the economic model and demand generation model, your business will have its unique and specific criteria for what constitutes a sales-qualified lead.

Like with the greater economic model, the demand generation model has its applicable ACV, churn, and repeat purchase rate. It also has three additional terms: fit rate, closing rate, and win rate.

Fit rate is based upon whatever your sales structure is (something we'll later discuss in Chapter 6: The Sales Model). How many qualified leads need to be touched to get to the opportunity where someone would buy from you?

As an example, if you're an eCommerce company your fit rate would be how many people who fit your profile end up visiting your website so that one of your visitors puts something in their shopping cart.

If you are a field sales organization, your fit rate would be the number of companies that fit your profile which your sales rep talks to in order to make a proposal. In terms of steps, your fit rate reflects the first to the second-to-last step of your sales process.

The last step is buying, which brings us to the **closing rate**. This number reflects the distance from your penultimate step to the last step. From the proposal to the buy.

Let's say I need to talk to five companies to get to the point where I'm making a full, bonafide proposal for one of the companies to buy from me. This means I've got a 20 percent fit rate. Then, the closing rate would be for one of the companies that get to the second-to-last step to actually buy. If I need to make three proposals to get one buy, my closing rate would be 33 percent.

The **win rate** is what takes me from the very first step to the very last step, and it's basically:

Fit rate × Closing rate

In the example where I have to talk to five companies to get to a proposal, and I need to make three proposals to win one, then my win rate is roughly 6.7 percent, or 20 percent times 33 percent.

After I've calculated my fit rate, closing rate, and win rate, I would know that sales needs to be able to connect with 15 companies that fit our profile for us to generate one customer.

CRUNCHING REAL NUMBERS

After talking about so many hypotheticals, it's time for a real-life example so you can see these elements of the economic model in practice. The following two-part story is based on real data, although I've changed the names and extraneous details to protect the privacy of the parties involved.

During the course of this story, rather than getting lost in the specific numbers, I want you to pay attention to the underlying mathematical relationships between the elements we've discussed.

BILBO BAGGINS AND THE DEMAND GENERATION MODEL

A while back, we were working with a two-year-old technology advisory and services company, which I'll call Bilbo Baggins & Co. (Yeah, I like *Lord of the Rings.*) This was a company looking for high growth. They completed their series A round three months before consulting us, raising $4 million. Having just hired a new head of sales, they were looking to get everything in place to drive a highly successful demand generation and sales effort. They just crossed a million-dollar annual run rate with a goal to hit $7 million in the next three years and a stretch goal of hitting $10 million.

	Scenario 1	Scenario 2	Scenario 3
Current Revenue	$ 1,000,000	$ 1,000,000	$ 1,000,000
Three-Year Goal	$ 7,000,000	$ 7,000,000	$ 7,000,000
Revenue Growth	$ 6,000,000	$ 6,000,000	$ 6,000,000
Average Client Size	$ 27,500	$ 27,500	$ 27,500
Churn	22%	15%	10%
New Revenue Needed	$ 8,196,426	$ 7,447,085	$ 6,460,254
New Customers Needed	298	271	235
Closing Rate	33%	33%	40%
Proposals Needed	903	281	588
Fit Rate	25%	33%	33%
Sales Qualified Leads	3,612	2,489	1,780

Their current revenue was $1 million dollars, and they told us their three-year target was $7 million. Their ACV was $27,500, and they had a 22 percent churn rate, a 33 percent closing rate, and a 25 percent fit rate.

With those numbers, getting from $1 million to $7 million in three years and achieving a net growth of $6 million would require Bilbo Baggins to generate far more than $6 million of new business. Remember, they were losing on average 22 percent of their business every year.

So the first thing we did was calculate how much more the company needed to generate to hit their $6 million in three years goal. It came out to around $8.2 million; the actual number was $8,196,426. If everything about their current economic model held true, that's how much new revenue they would need to generate to be at $7 million in three years.

What did this mean for their sales team? Well, with an ACV of $27,500, they would need to generate 298 new customers over those three years. With a 33 percent closing rate, they would need to deliver just over 900 proposals, and their sales team would have to generate 3,612 sales-qualified leads.

Sounds a little ambitious, but not impossible, right? Well, at the time we began working with Bilbo Baggins & Co., their total customer base was 36.

I see this pattern all the time in funded and non-funded companies, where the natural approach that people take is to put the pedal to the metal and run, run, run, run, run. But remember, speed alone will not get you where you need to be to achieve growth. By understanding the demand generation model, we can increase the efficacy—the velocity—of our strategy.

For example, what if we improved Bilbo Baggins' marketing efforts so instead of a 25 percent fit rate, they had a 33 percent fit rate? By taking the fit rate from 25 percent to 33 percent, we could decrease the number of sales-qualified leads they needed to generate by nearly a third, from 3,612 to 2,489. We decreased the number of proposals needed by roughly 10 percent.

Now, if we worked on better sales training, clearer messaging, and improving the overall sales process, we could get from a 33 percent close rate to a 40 percent close rate. By focusing less on speed and more on efficacy, the company could cut the numbers that they would need to generate by 40 percent.

When you understand your demand generation model, you can run different calculated scenarios to establish a hypothesis, to be able to test what you're doing, and to guide the actions that you're taking. Without that understanding, you're throwing spaghetti against the wall and seeing what sticks.

BILBO BAGGINS AND THE ECONOMIC MODEL

Based upon the conversations that we had with Bilbo Baggins & Co., and realizing that their churn rate was too high, we began to focus on developing the acquisition element of their economic model.

Their gross margin was 82 percent. We targeted getting their churn down to 15 percent, which meant they had a seven-year average lifetime. We set 25 percent for the cost of customer acquisition. If the company could achieve its objective, which meant they were going to add 271 new customers that were going to pay on average $27,500 at an 82 percent margin, their gross profit would be $22,550 with an average lifetime of seven years. That meant every customer Bilbo Baggins' acquired was worth $160,000; the actual number was $157,850.

As a side note, if you've ever watched *Shark Tank*, one of the most often asked asset test questions is "What's it cost to acquire a customer?" The people who answer it clearly have a chance to move forward. And I don't think anyone who has failed to answer that question has ever gotten funded on that show. That's how important understanding your acquisition cost is.

Now, if I offered a stock or bond that would give you $160,000 over the next seven years, would you be willing to invest in it? If yes, what would you pay me for it? Probably not $160,000, right?

If you looked at it through the lens of pure economics, every average customer the company got under the new economic model would be worth $160,000. Now, the difference between buying a bond and going to market is that the risk is much higher getting the $160,000 through business. And so this is where that question comes into play.

Based on the target that we set (235 new customers), we distributed it across their three-year timeline, so they were looking at a year one target of 39 additional customers, a year two target of 78 customers, and a year three target of 118 customers.

In year one, generating 39 new customers at a valuation of $160,000 gross profit, that amount of new business would be worth approximately $6.15 million. In total, the 235 customers would basically generate an asset base worth $37 million. And if you're going after something that's worth $37 million, chances are you're going to face some pretty steep competition for that asset.

This is why you need to ask:

How much am I willing to pay?

Bilbo Baggins & Co. was willing to spend 25 percent of the lifetime value of a customer to acquire said customer, which meant they would be willing to spend $40,000 ($39,462.50 is the exact number) to acquire a customer valued at $160,000. For the total of 235 customers, that was nearly $9.3 million in acquisition costs.

Let's narrow down the window a bit to just year one. Year one is worth $6.2 million, and that meant that Bilbo Baggins & Co. needed to be prepared to spend $1.5 million to acquire that 6.2 million.

Now, it might seem simple to say, "Hey, I wanna generate 39 new customers!" because that doesn't sound like a lot, does it?

From a revenue standpoint in this story, that's the same as saying you're going to generate a million dollars of revenue (39 customers at $27,500 each). It's easy to say 39 customers. It's easy to say, "We're going to generate a million dollars of revenue." But you're not really looking to generate just a million dollars of revenue. You're looking to generate a million dollars of revenue that's going to repeat for years.

This gets to my favorite quote of all time from Joe Lewis, who said, "Everybody wants to go to heaven, but nobody wants to die."

It's easy to define what you want to get. The real question is, what are you willing to pay to get it?

TIPS AND TAKEAWAYS

In Chapter 5, we discussed the second element of the go-to-market approach: the economic model. While the specifics of your economic model are unique to your business, there are a few important aspects to remember:

- Make clear choices and trade-off decisions to strengthen your go-to-market approach,
- An effective economic model requires an understanding of the mathematical underpinnings of smaller elements, such as acquisition, lifetime value, and demand generation,
- To define demand generation, you must define and differentiate your leads,
- And you must know what you're willing to pay before you know what you are able to acquire.

Few people like math, but most businesses like growth. So, whether you like it or not, whether you calculate it or not, the math is going to matter. That's the heart of the economic model, and why it's one of the most fundamental components of a successful go-to-market approach.

CHAPTER 6

THE SALES MODEL

DAVID SMITH, OWNER OF SMITH ELECTRONICS, WAS TRYING TO solve a problem. His revenues were growing, but his profits and margins were not.

He attempted to solve this problem by hiring more salespeople. But the net result of that was more internal chaos and disruption and higher costs. Sure, sales and revenue were growing, but revenue per rep was a negative trend. The only "positive" trend seemed to be the growing cost per customer acquisition and retention.

David's problem wasn't a lack of sales capacity. In fact, our analysis indicated that his "fully-utilized" sales team was only producing 55 to 65 percent of the economic impact that it should have.

David's problem was the sales model. He was playing the wrong game with the wrong type of people.

When talking about sales and sales approaches, I often like to ask people, "Who is the greatest football player of all time?" After getting a blank stare for a couple of seconds, and sometimes a look of "what the hell does that have to do with sales?", people will eventually tell me who their favorite player is or who they think is the best player of all time. I'll often get a "Jim Brown" or a "Walter Payton." If they're from

New England, they might even say, "Tom Brady." I almost always get the name of a star quarterback, running back, or wide receiver.

My follow-up question is, "What if you were looking for a left tackle? Would they still be the greatest football players of all time?" And my point on sales is made.

CHOOSING YOUR SALES MODEL

Your sales model, or sales structure, is the element of your go-to-market approach that gets at the machine that enables you to generate customers and generate revenue.

There are basically three types of sales models. The first sales model is what I call the self-serve (or unassisted) model. This is where the customer buys on their own. If your business is in eCommerce, you're most likely using a self-serve sales model. As another example, grocery stores can operate under a self-serve sales model. No salesperson is involved; there is no one explaining to you the features and benefits of a box of cereal. And, increasingly, you don't need someone to cash you out at the register.

The second is the rep-assisted model. This is also a generally self-driven model, which is becoming increasingly prevalent in today's online market space. However, unlike the first model, the rep-assisted sales model is used for businesses that will often require a person to get involved with the customer's experience, whether that is to answer a question or help customers get things across the finish line. A rep-assisted sale lowers the threshold, though typically a rep-assisted sale can still handle more volume compared to the third sales model.

The third is the rep-directed model, where a sales rep is leading the process. Sometimes the only model that has a chance of working is a rep-directed model. I see this happen all the time. People have a great idea with a relatively low price point. It could be an absolutely wonderful idea, but because it's so new or niche or different, it requires a lot of explanation. It requires human involvement and sales reps to really initiate and direct the sales of the product. I see a lot of small businesses get trapped when they don't understand their economic model before they've defined what their sales model is going to be. When the economic model doesn't support the sales model that you have, and if there's a misalignment between your economic model and your sales model, the economic model's going to win every time.

CHOOSING YOUR BUSINESS ANGLE

A great exercise that you can do, regardless of your model, is to imagine a future where, for whatever reason, no person is allowed to touch an opportunity directly. Every one of your sales would need to become self-serve or unassisted. How would you do it? With a truly rep-directed sales model, you wouldn't be able to answer that question fully, but it's still a wonderful exercise for revenue operations people and senior leaders to do. This thought exercise gets you to identify how you can better utilize the people in your organization. Far too often, we're assigning people to do things even when they're not the best choice for the task.

The second part of the sales model is the two angles of new business and existing business (or the land and expand, respectively). A land portion of the sales model is where you have salespeople focused on new business and new customers only. The other reps responsible for managing customers and growing that customer base belong to the expand side. Some people do both, and this also applies to companies as a whole. A manufacturing company, for example, might provide materials for a contract over a set period of time. There really is no expand element here. They win the business, they get the contract, and it's done. That's a land business. There are other businesses where you want to start small with somebody and then grow that customer. This is where you would follow a path of land and expand.

So the first choice question you need to ask yourself about your sales model is, "Are you a self-serve, rep-assisted, or rep-directed?" The second question should be, "Are you a land or land and expand?" And if you decide your model is a land and expand, don't leave the "expand" part of the sales model up to chance. I see far too many companies, especially service companies, that will underprice their land because they think,

"We'll win this business. Then, we're going to do such a good job that they're going to want to do even more business with us!" I'm not saying that never happens, but I wouldn't bank my future on a land and expand model without having a clear path for both motions.

CHOOSING YOUR STRUCTURE

Understanding your business angle will also help you determine the third aspect of your sales model—the structure.

For the sales model, we basically have four structures, and the first of those four is what I refer to as the traditional structure. Within the traditional structure, sales reps are "full cycle" reps. They handle things from the beginning to the end. They find the new customers, and they win the customers. The rep is involved in the process all the way through. The mentality within the traditional structure is, "This is my account. These are my customers."

As companies grow, they tend to become territory-based or product-line-based operations, and regions begin to develop. It's a pretty straightforward structure where, as you get bigger, management begins to introduce more and more roles like sales manager, sales director, and so on. With the traditional sales structure, the organization within sales is going to look like your typical pyramid.

The second form of sales structure is the specialized structure. Here, the roles of sales are broken up. The most common specialization of roles happens when an organization is differentiating between generating new business and managing existing customers. Within a specialized structure, you will end up with common roles like account executives and account managers. Separate from that are the dedicated prospecting roles, typically referred to as sales development.

Unlike the traditional structure where one rep handles every task from beginning to end, you instead have people specialized to a specific function along the sales cycle. Despite the difference in how roles and functions within sales are allocated, a specialized structure tends to also have a pyramid-like organization from a management standpoint.

Larger companies, normally those dealing with more complexity, will trend toward **matrix structures**. In a matrix organization, roles are viewed through the lens of vertical and horizontal responsibilities. Say a company has 17 different product lines. There is a high degree of specialization for each of those product lines, but there is also a high degree of cross-pollination, or cross-sale. Most customers use multiple product lines. This would be a case where horizontal specialization alone wouldn't be enough, so adding a vertical element—basically, creating a matrix of roles—would be favorable.

An excellent real-world example of a matrix organization would be Merrill Lynch, a huge company that offers investments, insurances, mortgages, corporate banking, and so on and so forth. Because of the combination of the company size, diversity of product line, and high probability of cross-sale, Merrill Lynch's reps operated according to horizontal and vertical specialized roles. When I was working there years ago, I would have categorized myself as one of the horizontal reps, though within the company, I was called a financial advisor, or sometimes a wealth management advisor. Regardless of title, my job was to manage the customers according to a "land and expand" business angle.

Then, there were the reps that were in the vertical component of the matrix. A majority of our vertical roles were fulfilled by people working as insurance specialists and corporate banking specialists. Each of those specialists was part of their own organization within the larger organization of Merrill Lynch. In many ways, to the vertical reps, I was as much of a prospect as my own customers were. Whenever I would come across someone who seemed like a good candidate for insurance, I would get the vertical reps involved. To understand and be able to represent everything within a specialized role was more than you can ask a horizontal rep to do, so that's where I would bring in a vertical rep to fulfill the role of, in this case, "insurance specialist."

The last structure is what I'll refer to as an integrated structure. That's where you're actually bringing together multiple elements from the previous three structures. So, for an integrated structure, you might have specialization and vertical/horizontal differentiation of rep roles, but there's another added element: instead of looking at sales through the lens of chopping up a process, you look at your sales structure as a method of breaking up roles into their fundamental Jobs to Be Done.

Head of Sales

	Vertical 1	Vertical 2	Vertical 3	Solution Design
	Leader	Leader	Leader	Solution Designers (Provokers) Solution Architects
Account Executives (The Engagers)	Reps	Reps	Reps	
Leader — Marketing Development (The Finders)	Reps	Reps	Reps	
Leader — Channel & Partnerships	Reps			

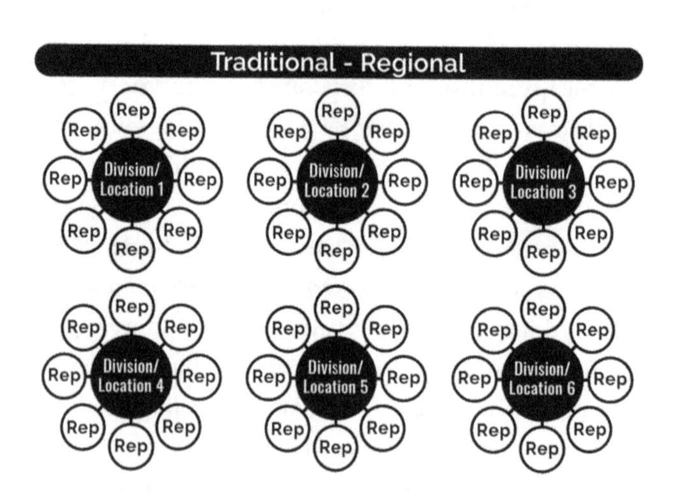

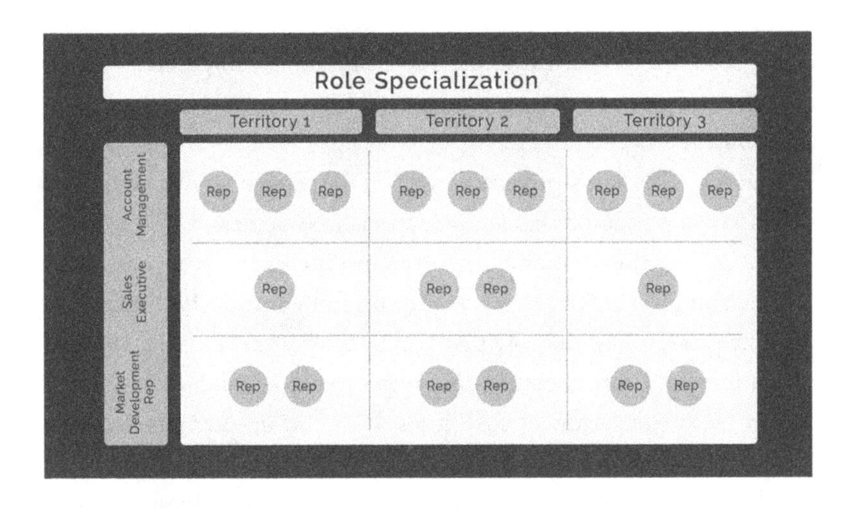

Matrix

Line/Focus 1
Line/Focus 2
Line/Focus 3
Line/Focus 4
Line/Focus 5

Challenger Rep
New Sales SME Account Executive
Account Manager | Engager-Expander
Market Development Rep

Rep

ADVANTAGES AND DISADVANTAGES OF THE FOUR SALES STRUCTURES

The advantage of the traditional sales structure is that it's simple. It's the least expensive model, but that can also be a disadvantage. Increasingly, traditional structures don't stand up to the complexities and needs of today's world. They don't stand up to how buyers buy. If you're dealing in complex competitive environments (which is every competitive market environment nowadays), this type of structure lacks the resiliency and the robustness needed to excel.

The specialization structure allows you to increase productivity. But there's a major trade-off: For a purely specialized element to work, there will be an increased volume, so you're also increasing your cost. The volume and productivity that you pick up from a specialized structure must be greater than the cost that you take on from adopting the specialization. And this structure does require stronger alignment efforts within the organization so customers don't end up experiencing the frustration of being handed off from one rep to another to the next. Another limitation of the specialized structure is that it doesn't handle much complexity. It's the right direction to go for a traditional organization that is seeing faster growth or has outgrown its initial, basic needs, but a specialized sales structure doesn't really reach the far end of more complex demand generation.

In contrast, the matrix structure can handle more complexity because of its horizontal and vertical role specialization. It is a structure that allows you to orient and align with your customers better, which makes hiring for sales roles easier because you segment out which tasks each salesperson is needed for. Much like traditional structures, the matrix's advantage is also its disadvantage. To handle more complexity, the structure itself is more complex. From a cost standpoint, each level of structure we talk about is more robust than the last. So if I'm selling a low-margin product, a matrix structure would bankrupt me. It's more difficult to manage than the first two structures, and if you're not careful, you can lose accountability.

Finally, with the integrated structure, its biggest advantage is that it is the most robust, most resilient structure for any organization. If scaling growth and sustaining growth is the direction you want to go, this is the structure that can withstand the high level of complex demand generation. But as you've probably guessed, and given the trade-offs of the other three sales structures, a high degree of integration requires a high degree of complexity and stronger processes and data to manage.

TIPS AND TAKEAWAYS

In Chapter 6, we discussed the third element of a successful go-to-market approach: the sales model. When it comes to constructing an appropriate sales model for your business, there are a few key choices you must make once you have determined:

- How your business generates its customers and revenue (sales model),
- Whether you are revenue goals are oriented toward sustaining, growth, or both (business angle),
- And the degree of complexity of the sales roles carried out by your reps (sales structures).

"Sales" is one of those words that gets tossed around by a lot of different people to describe lots of different roles and lots of different approaches. But just like the rest of the components of a successful go-to-market approach, your sales model is only as effective as your ability to accurately define the revenue goals of your business.

CHAPTER 7

MESSAGING, POSITIONING, AND NARRATIVE

BEFORE WE JUMP INTO THIS CHAPTER, I WANT YOU TO PAUSE AND think about how much time, money, energy, and effort your business expends just to differentiate itself from your competitors. My bet is, it's a lot.

Now, ask yourself, "How much are my competitors expending to differentiate themselves from me?" I'd also bet it's a lot.

And while you're doing a bunch of things over here and your competitors are doing a whole bunch over there, do you know what customers call all of that work? Do you know what customers call the effort that everybody in your market is expending to catch their intent to buy? They call it noise. The net result of all your work is that customers spend less and less time trying to understand what makes each company different, what makes *you* different. What's left is commoditization.

Years ago I made an observation that completely changed how I think about key principles in marketing, like differentiation. I realize that the people and organizations who are really different, never seem to have to tell people that they're different.

Michael Jordan doesn't introduce himself to people by saying, "Hi, I'm Michael Jordan, and I'm one of the greatest basketball players of all time." He doesn't have to tell you he's a great basketball player. You realize it immediately. If anything, it's the person who does come up and introduce themselves as great or unique that leaves you thinking "There's something wrong here." In our day-to-day lives, we've all probably met a person who boasts about how great they are when we know (and maybe even they know) they're not that good.

Your messaging, positioning, and narrative will determine whether people see your business as a resource to achieve their desired outcomes, or as just another bit of noise.

NOBODY CARES ABOUT YOUR STUFF

When I'm working with clients on the go-to-market messaging and positioning, I ask them this question: If I had ten good, qualified prospects for your business and all ten prospects made the right decision, the right way, as defined by you, how many of those prospects would buy?

I've asked hundreds of companies that question, and I've gotten thousands of responses from the people participating. Ninety percent of the time, they either struggle to give a clear number or say something along the lines of, "as few as two and as many as five."

The answer *should be* a clear, confident ten. Think about it. If all ten prospects made the right decision, the right way, as defined by you, then why wouldn't they all buy from you? If that's not the case, you might want to put this book down for now. You've got bigger problems to solve than revenue acceleration.

If *you* don't even believe your products are the right choice for the right people, then who should?

After a short discussion where my client comes to realize that this wasn't a trick question, I'll ask them what the point of the example is. The answer is that the key to influencing your customers' purchase decisions is to stop focusing on your products or services, and instead to put that effort towards teaching them how to make the right decision, the right way.

Early in my sales career, I had a coach who shared with me that everyone in the world wakes up with the same goal in mind. Then he asked me if I wanted to know what that goal was. Of course, I was eager for the answer. He replied, "They don't want to meet you."

I asked him what he meant. He replied, "Who's sitting around with extra time thinking, 'If only a salesperson would introduce themselves to me so I can buy something.' Doug, you have to realize nobody, except for *maybe* you, cares about or wants your shit! They care about themselves, their problems, and their goals and dreams. They're trying to figure their world out, and if you want to resonate with them, if you want to influence them, you'll focus on their issues, not yours."

In most cases with an unsuccessful go-to-market approach, the real problem isn't sales, revenue, or growth—it's a messaging problem. Simply put, your message isn't relevant to your market.

MESSAGING

Great companies define and align behind a very clear message, something that I like to call a "point of view" message. In other words, they deliver a strong point of view. A strong point of view message is one that people can and will disagree with. Some people get nervous about taking too strong of a stance for their own business or products. It might not feel great to know your point of view message is ruffling some feathers. But you have to understand that not everyone needs your product, and an effective message should focus on capturing the attention of those who do need your product. If you've only got a mild, middle-of-the-road message that nobody can muster up the interest to disagree with, then nobody is really going to agree with it either.

A clear point of view message is one that focuses on your prospect's world. Your message should make a connection to an important or critical issue for your prospect. It should challenge their thinking. You're not looking to agree with your prospect because a lot of prospects may come with a stance of, "Why do I have to buy? I'm happy where I am." Replying to that with "I agree. You don't have to buy. But you could buy" is not a strong point of view message. It's a mixed message. An effective point of view message should course-correct. It's not supposed to distract prospects from their destinations; it should help them get to their destination. And if your product isn't something that can help them do that, then you're not playing to your area of advantage. In essence, your message should be clear, prospect-oriented, and polarizing.

This leads us to the five components of a strong message. The first component is **simplicity**. Is your story simple? I call this the tennis ball theory of communication. Picture this: I toss one tennis ball to you. You could probably catch that. Now I toss three or more tennis balls at you, all at once. You probably wouldn't be able to catch them. The biggest messaging mistake I see happen again and again and again is sellers and marketers generate messaging that competes with itself for the buyers' attention. It's communicating too much. A simple story aligns to a single point, a single idea, and focuses on communicating that idea effectively.

The second element of a powerful message is it's **emotional**. By emotional, I don't mean that it's filled with adjectives or puffery. I mean that it tells a story. Humans are story-based creatures. We think in stories, we remember stories, and we project ourselves into stories.

We're all in the storytelling business, and I've learned that whoever tells the best story usually wins. So when you're telling a story, take a moment and ask yourself, "*Whose* story am I telling, exactly?" Because if you want to sell, then you should be telling the customer's story, not your own; never forget your customer.

The third element is that the message is **concrete**. Great communication is not about communicating so that you can be understood. That's the easy part; if you throw enough spaghetti at the wall, some of it will stick. The real mark of great communication is communicating so you can't be misunderstood. Make a promise. Be clear. Avoid allusions to promises that you can't keep, or vague platitudes. This not only ensures that the right people are hearing the right message, but that everyone else doesn't feel duped by a misinterpretation of features and promises that you didn't intend to make.

The fourth element is **context**. If I am your customer, don't tell me what you do or what you're selling. Tell me how it impacts me in relation to the results that I want. A strong story creates a GPS for the people that you're trying to attract. They have their destination—desired results—and you have the route—your product—that will get them there.

Fifth, a strong story is **polarizing.** It not only attracts the right people, it repels the wrong people. If I can't hate your message, I can't love your message. If I can't hate your story, I can't love your story.

AN ABSOLUTELY, POSITIVELY GREAT SLOGAN

Probably the greatest commercial message of all time is: When it absolutely, positively has to be there overnight. FedEx.

It's simple. It tells a story. It can't be misunderstood. It changed the world. And it was deeply polarizing.

When FedEx first came out, it was like $75 to send a letter. I remember someone asked me rhetorically, "Who would ever use Federal Express? That's so ridiculous. You know, the only people that would ever do that are people who aren't prepared and wait too long to get things done."

And I remember thinking to myself, "Yeah, I know. That's awesome! Now I can delay for like three more days." Obviously, my friend was never going to be FedEx's customer. They weren't the right person; but I was.

STORY AND NARRATIVE

So, clear and polarizing messaging gets put together into a strong story, and the strong story creates a great narrative. Every great story tells a narrative, but not just any narrative. A great story is like a children's bedtime story.

I remember reading stories to my children (when they would let me read to them). The stories were visual, they had a point of view, they taught lessons, and they were easy to remember.

An effective exercise for anyone in sales, marketing, or customer success is to write your story like it's a children's book. Break it down into simpler components. Every great narrative has a hero. Every great narrative has a guide. There's always a problem or an enemy, and it ends with a transformational outcome.

I'll use the narrative of *Star Wars* (which in my opinion is the greatest children's story of all time) to demonstrate:

The **hero** is Luke Skywalker.

The **guide** is Yoda.

The **enemy** is the dark force, the Death Star.

The **transformation** is the Rebels' victory.

For you, the hero is always your market, so your customer is Luke Skywalker. You are Yoda. Always remember that you are the guide and stop trying to make yourself Luke Skywalker. The issues and all the things discussed around providing a clear and polarizing message and story are your enemies. It's the problems and factors that have led to your hero working with you to solve. The transformational outcome is how you deliver the unique and key outcomes that you deliver.

Remember that your message is a commercial one, and so are the story and narrative you build around it. You aren't telling a story for fun. You're setting a stage so the right audience can hear the right message. Think of yourself as the right message and think of the right audience as customers who can reframe their situations, problems, or opportunities to ultimately buy from you. With an effective point of view message, you can construct a strong story and a great narrative for your go-to-market approach.

TIPS AND TAKEAWAYS

In Chapter 7, we covered the fourth element of a successful go-to-market approach: the messaging, positioning, and narrative of your business. To fulfill this part of your business's approach, it is important to remember:

- Great companies can deliver a clear "point-of-view" message,
- The strongest stories are those whose message cannot be misconstrued,
- And you are the guide, not the hero, of your business's narrative.

If there is only one thing you take from this chapter, it should be this:

There are no boring companies, only boring stories.

At the end of the day, the way you construct and deliver your narrative determines whether or not potential buyers will trust your business as a resource to fulfill their own needs. The story that you tell is not only that of your business, but that of your customers. Just like how a story cannot progress without a protagonist, your go-to-market approach cannot progress without a clear understanding of the customers who are central to your narrative.

PART III

STRUCTURE

CHAPTER 8

WHAT IS STRUCTURE

FEBRUARY 5, 2017. THE ATLANTA FALCONS WERE LEADING THE New England Patriots by a score of 28 to 3. Only 4 minutes and 49 seconds were left in the third quarter. One of the announcers, Cris Collinsworth, shakes his head. "The Patriots don't seem to be acting with any urgency. What's going on?"

In retrospect, we know that the Patriots came back and beat the Falcons with a final score of 34 to 28.

But as I was watching the Patriots win their fifth Super Bowl, what struck me about the experience wasn't the game itself. It wasn't that they came back to tie and beat the Falcons during overtime. What was most memorable to me was the behavior of the Patriots' head coach, Bill Belichick. When asked by reporters, "Were you ever worried you were going to lose?" Belichick simply said something to the effect of, "We never doubted that we were gonna win. The only question we had was if we were going to run out of time before we did."

At the end of the day, you can control what you do, but you can't control the outcome of what you do. While everybody else saw the scoreboard as 28 to 3, a projection of the Patriots' inevitable loss, the Patriots only saw the scoreboard as a manifestation of what had already happened, not an indication of what was going to happen next. That's why there was no major panic or sense of urgency from the team. What Belichick and his team knew was that everything they did, including their plays when they were behind 28 to 3, was precisely what they needed to do to continue their trajectory toward victory.

GALL'S LAW

In business, it is impossible to fully define and fully understand the structure and underlying systems that exist in any given situation. There are always challenges. There are always unexpected consequences. But the objective of strategic RevOps for an organization looking to scale growth is to be as purposeful as possible and to define the elements of your structure so that you increase the likelihood of people making decisions the way you want those decisions to be made.

When we're building structure and designing systems, we cannot jump the gun and go straight for the most complex system possible. According to Gall's Law, a complex system that works is invariably found to have evolved from a simple system that worked. The inverse of that is also true. A complex system designed from scratch to be a complex system will never work. It cannot be made to work.

To build a complex system, you have to start with a simple system. Consider the car. This complex system didn't start out as a "car." It didn't begin with the idea of transportation. The system started from something as simple as a "wheel." Over hundreds of thousands of iterations later, the simplest systems became complicated.

From a market-facing, revenue acceleration perspective, there are three primary elements of your structure that you need to focus on. Those elements are the system design, the tech stack, and the scoreboard.

THE INVISIBLE HAND

I think of structure as the invisible hand that guides everything.

Humans are funny creatures. We like to think we're in control and fully aware of our motives and actions. From a social and scientific standpoint, we are always trying to explain why other people do things or think the way that they do. In sales and marketing, this prevalent thought has led to a persistent structural flaw in businesses. CEOs and salespeople alike mistakenly view sales and marketing as behavioral disciplines. On the surface, that seems to be a no-brainer. Managing behavior is how we change behavior, right?

Well, plenty of organizations, in and out of the business world, have attempted to take that simple and direct approach to improve the productivity of their members. But it turns out that managing behaviors is not an effective approach to producing sustainable, repeatable, and scalable outcomes.

As Jonathan Haidt, author of *The Righteous Mind,* once said, "Our conscious mind likes to think of itself as the Oval Office, when in reality it's the press office." We like to think we're in control of what we do. We like to think that our conscious minds are issuing orders. But really, we're just retroactively rationalizing our impulses and subconscious motivations. One of the first lessons I learned in sales is that people don't buy logically. They buy emotionally and justify it with logic. That's really how people make decisions.

"Humans are not logical creatures who sometimes feel; we're feeling creatures who occasionally think."

—BRENÉ BROWN

Humans are creatures who dwell on the path of least resistance. Or, simply: we're lazy. So, understanding the structure that people operate within is going to help us to understand the decisions people make, how they make those decisions, and how they will likely respond to the consequences of those decisions.

When you can identify your organization's underlying structure and incentives, you can more effectively influence the RevOps and growth outcomes of your people's behaviors.

STRUCTURE AND ITS KEY ELEMENTS

In this overview, we've discussed the invisible hand as the philosophy of structure. In the following chapters, we'll discuss the conscious, successful execution of three elements of structure: system design, tech stacks, and the scoreboard.

While we are breaking things down for the purpose of understanding each element better, make no mistake about the nature of structure. "Structure" is not a group of parts, but the bigger picture—the dynamic between system design, tech, and the scoreboard is what creates the whole.

TIPS AND TAKEAWAYS

In Chapter 8, we covered the role of structure as the invisible guide of human behavior. When building structure for your business, it is important to remember the additional key points of:

- Building a great complex system from a good simple system,
- Remembering that humans are not purely logical creatures, but feeling creatures who occasionally think,
- And understanding that structure is not only made of its elements, but the relationship those elements have with each other.

Structure is the invisible hand that guides all actions. Structure creates incentives, and incentives drive behavior. In the following chapters, we will cover the importance of conscious decision-making and the elements of system design, tech stacks, and the scoreboard to create an effective, incentivizing structure for your business.

CHAPTER 9

SYSTEM DESIGN

"You do not rise to the level of your goals. You fall to the level of your systems."

—JAMES CLEAR, *Atomic Habits*

The goal of a strong system design is knowing when (and how) to solve your problems upstream and downstream. In other words, know the difference between fire prevention and firefighting, and have both. This requires you to build the genius into the system.

I used to present a popular workshop to CEO groups on scaling business growth. In the workshop, I would ask the question, "How many of you would define your sales organizational experience as producing consistent results at or above expectations with limited disruption and few surprises?" Usually, only one or two out of every ten CEOs would raise their hands. There's a good reason for that, though it might not be the one you're expecting.

The traditional approach to sales organizations is designed to produce inconsistent, disruptive, all-over-the-place outcomes with lots of surprises. You see, if I asked that question and nine out of ten CEOs raised their hands and said, "My company sees consistent results, limited disruption, and few surprises," then my workshop would be totally different. I'd instead look at the one CEO who didn't raise their hand and think, "Oh, that one CEO's got a sales problem, or a behavioral problem." But it's the complete opposite.

When only one in ten CEOs raises their hand, that's indicative of an overarching problem with traditional system design and sales. It is no longer an individualistic, surface-level issue. If you want to change the outcome of sales, you must change its underlying systems and structure.

Building the genius into the system means designing a system that does a lot of the thinking. It takes average to above-average people and unlocks their talent. A well-designed system frees your salespeople to perform at their best instead of becoming another thing to be actively managed and accounted for by sales.

I remember this old commercial for Fram oil filters, where the oil filter guy would say, "You can pay me now or you can pay me later." And what happens as you pick up complexity, as businesses grow? More and more things happen downstream, right? That's what creates a lot of drag and a lot of bad friction.

FRICTION, FLYWHEELS, AND TAXES

The second law of thermodynamics says that entropy is always increasing. (Yes. We are getting into thermodynamics in a book about revenue acceleration.)

Entropy is disorder and randomness. In clearer terms, it means that within any system or structure, disorder and randomness are always increasing. It's important to understand that increasing disorder is the natural state. In your business, this disorder manifests itself as friction. You can say that friction is the entropy of business. As your business grows, or simply survives, it will pick up more complexity. That complexity creates friction. Before long, what seemed easy becomes very, very difficult, or even impossible to sustain.

The natural state of entropy isn't limited to physics or business, either. During my kids' first years in college, they introduced me to a new term called "adulting." Do you know what you have to do to experience adulting? You just have to live for about 18 years, sometimes less than that, and you'll eventually have to deal with adulting. From a life standpoint, as we've gotten older, our lives have gotten more complex. There are more things that we have to do. More decisions that we have to make. That's another example of the natural state.

So when your business exists, even under ordinary, sustaining operations, friction inevitably increases. When growth is a primary objective, you are basically lighting a match beside the gasoline of friction, multiplying the friction you must manage. The challenge that most organizations face is their rate of complexity is growing at a faster rate than their ability to manage the complexity. This is why system design is crucial to success—focusing on the resulting behaviors is not sufficient, because that only addresses the symptoms and not the causes of friction.

The key to sustaining growth and making growth manageable and predictable (and even enjoyable) boils down to how you manage complexity to reduce the negative friction that it causes. For simplicity's sake, visualize the management of friction like a flywheel. A popular metaphor for the dynamics of growing and scaling a business is the flywheel, and my favorite example of a business growth flywheel was put together by HubSpot. The three elements of HubSpot's flywheel are as follows: Attract. Engage. Delight.

The better you are at attracting the right types of people, the more likely they are to engage with your message, products, and services, to ultimately buy them. And as you get better at engaging with buyers and delivering the products and services they're looking for, they're more likely to be happy. The happier they are with your products and services, the more likely they are to talk about you and post about you through their social media, which will then make it easier for you to attract more people, which will make it easier for you to engage, which will make it easier for you to delight...and so on and so forth. As you improve upon each aspect of the process, it reinforces and propels itself, and you will pick up speed. What started off hard early on becomes easier over time and you can accelerate more without depleting your organization of its vital resources. That's the flywheel.

Historically, executives have only been able to work on one part of the flywheel to increase its momentum. Their only play was to increase the force to push the flywheel faster. They apply more and more force for the flywheel to go faster. Do more, do it better, do it faster, and do it with fewer resources. That's been the battle cry for most businesses over the last 50 years, and it's exactly why everyone's so tired today. It's why we're seeing the social fabric fraying. We've increased force to the point where it's not sustainable. But there's another part to the flywheel that far too many organizations miss. Instead of wondering, "How do I apply more force to the flywheel," you should be asking:

What can I do to reduce the friction in the flywheel?

As you do more, you ultimately hit the point of diminishing returns. Increasing force will eventually hit the wall of ineffectiveness. You don't experience that when reducing friction. Here's a simple example. Let's say you're trying to see how many times you can spin a quarter. You set it up on a table and flick it as hard as you can. The harder you flick it, the faster it initially turns. That's increasing force. Now imagine that you took that quarter to outer space, where there is very little friction. How much force would you have to use to flick that quarter and have it spin ten times longer than before? Surprisingly little force, actually.

Reducing friction provides a high degree of leverage to your organization.

The only way to execute at scale is to address the barriers, conflicts, gaps, confusions, and ambiguity that impact your organization before those issues hit the point of execution. That's what eliminating friction is about. So whenever one of these barnacles gets added on, whenever one of these issues presents itself, it creates friction, and your company pays what I will refer to as a "friction tax."

To date, I've analyzed over one thousand companies, and here are our findings:

The best companies, those that are the best at system design and addressing the issues we've discussed in this book, pay roughly 10 to 15 percent in what I call the friction tax. I should mention here it's impossible *not* to pay a friction tax. As they say, there are only two things guaranteed in life: death and taxes. Well, one of those taxes is friction.

Good companies typically pay a tax of 33 to 45 percent and average companies pay more than 50 percent in friction tax. That means the average companies are losing half of the impact of their efforts for growth. Put another way, they're working twice as hard for half as much.

The latest research from CSO showed that salespeople were spending just over 30 percent of their time actually selling. That's the average number, so let's assume the salespeople in your business are spending 30 percent. What if, by redesigning your system and processes, you could increase the time they spent selling by just 3 percent? If someone spent 3 percent more time doing something than they had previously, the difference would be imperceptible. You wouldn't be able to tell the difference between a person spending 30 percent of their time selling and a person who's spending 33 percent of their time selling. But the person spending 33 percent of their time selling is getting 10 percent more yield.

Based on my company's research into the efficacy of reducing friction, the time that a business's salespeople spend selling should ideally be somewhere between 37.5 and 45 percent. That's what you should be shooting for. Imagine this: You have a team of salespeople spending 30 percent of their time selling, when a redesign of your system could have them spending 40 percent of their time selling. You've got 21 people in your team. If you could increase the percentage of their time from 30 percent to 40 percent, you just added the equivalent productivity of 7 people to your organization by reducing friction.

Big results come from small, almost imperceptible changes. I've seen hundreds of sales organizations at work, and a 2 to 5 percent increase at key inflection points led to 25, 35, and in some cases even 50 percent differences in the economic impact that the organizations produced. This was from a profitability standpoint, a growth standpoint, and an enterprise standpoint. So, accomplishing big things doesn't come from the big things that you do.

WHAT IS SYSTEM DESIGN?

Before I get further into the details of system design, understand that the word "system" itself can refer to many different things. Too often, when people hear the word system, they think of technology, because technology is a kind of system. But what we're talking about is the bigger, broader system. The system we will be referring to here is the design of all of the elements that are impacting the people in your organization as they move forward.

Additionally, system design is about addressing a principle I refer to as the "inverse friction" or "inverse complexity" principle. Everybody's objective is to make the user's experience as effortless as possible. What the inverse friction principle says is that "the ease of any user's experience in any situation is inverse to the difficulty, complexity, and effort of creating that effortless experience."

Furthermore, there's an important distinction to be made between complicated and complex systems. I see a lot of people who treat those terms as synonyms. In reality, they're not perfectly interchangeable.

A BUTTERFLY FLAPS ITS WINGS—THE DIFFERENCE BETWEEN COMPLICATED AND COMPLEX

There's an old phrase that describes chaos theory and complexity, and it goes like this: A butterfly flaps its wings in Australia, and it rains in Bangor, Maine. Complexity is interdependence.

Complicated refers to problems or situations that are difficult to address; but they *are* addressable. They've got rules, recipes, and heuristics. Oftentimes, their solutions involve algorithms. Complicated problems are really built for modern-day algorithms because they're designed to be solved. Complicated problems are problems that can be solved, and most likely should be solved. Building a powerful piece of technology is complicated, but it also has very clear rules. It has very clear patterns of cause-and-effect. Modern finance is complicated, but when done legally, it too has very clear rules. There's right and there's wrong. Complicated issues and complicated systems are typically independent.

They're closed loops. Your operation or your manufacturing process is a complicated system where you control all the inputs and outputs.

Complex problems and systems, on the other hand, involve too many interdependent issues, unknowns, and feedback loops to be perfectly understood. That unknowable factor makes procedures and even algorithms far less effective, even counterproductive. Complex problems, which are oftentimes also called "wicked problems," are problems that have no real solution. For example, poverty is a complex problem. When you change one element of the poverty problem, you're inadvertently changing so many other things that the situation you were solving for is no longer the situation that you are in.

One of the common problems (and why system design is so important to structure) is that we fall into the trap where complicated and complex are used interchangeably. But good system design requires us to differentiate between the two; a business is a *complex* ecosystem. We only control a portion, never the whole. Because there are so many interdependencies and so many things are changing at the same time, you can't really predict fully what's going to happen. There are causal elements, but it's not the same as defined cause-and-effects for complicated systems.

Complex systems are often representative of a multitude of interdependent systems that are impacting whatever the situation is we're trying to improve, or we're trying to address. The weather, for example, is a complex system. Complex problems need to be managed, because complex problems are never actually solved. The ongoing nature of complex problems is also why the work of growing an organization is never truly done.

Why does Steph Curry look like he's putting forth no effort as he sets new records for three-point shots? Watch how hard he works in practice.

Why is it so easy to order a ride or delivery through Uber? Look at how complex the underlying design of the application is.

Too often, in pursuit of simplicity, we simplify the system design itself. But that only offloads all of the complexity onto the execution, the user experience. A strong design addresses the complexity and reduces the task of managing friction within the system so that the user can perform better, with less interference and confusion.

THE PERFORMANCE IMPROVEMENT LOOP

An effective system design maximizes value creation within the constraints that exist for you and your organization. It's a forever ongoing process that has four recurring steps to it.

Step one, empathize. You cannot enhance, iterate, or improve your systems without a strong foundation of empathy. Empathy is all about having a comprehensive, holistic understanding of the situation, the inputs, the stakeholders, and the objectives. It's as complete of an understanding as you can reasonably get of what's going on within your organization. Empathizing is also about understanding the desired output and what the desired ideal would be. Understanding your system design requires a multi-discipline, multi-experience approach to get started.

Step two, hypothesize. To sustain improvement, you must be able to build a strong hypothesis about progress. This requires divergent thinking. You must be willing to break things apart and challenge previously held beliefs and assumptions. Unfortunately, humans are not naturally good at this. We seek confirmation. We pursue confirmation. We don't challenge our beliefs so much as we check to make sure we believe the "right" things. The most common and damaging mistake I see committed during a company's improvement efforts is the quick jump from identifying a potential problem to determining the solution. The problem you think you see is seldom the real problem.

Step three, analyze. With your hypotheses laid out, the next step is to analyze potential approaches and determine which ones fit best to get the job done. The analysis stage focuses on breaking down the various elements to ensure you address causes, as opposed to symptoms. Once you gain clarity on the upstream, sidestream, and downstream impact of the adjustments that you're considering, you can move on to testing the various approaches before determining which is the one you're going to commit to and pursue.

Step four, synthesize. Synthesizing is about bringing convergent thinking to the forefront. Step two was about divergence. Now, in the fourth step, we're bringing things together. The focus here is integrating the new adjustments into the current and existing processes. Synthesizing is a crucial final step in system design if you want to minimize or eliminate disruption. This stage is all about integrating the new with the current to enable everyone to adopt and accelerate.

Through the entire system designing process, you will also be managing three core trade-offs.

The first one is feasibility. Right off the bat, you should ask yourself, "Can we do this?" System design is about orchestrating the best path given the constraints that exist for you.

The next trade-off is viability. "Will we be able to sustain this?" A common mistake of skipping system design in favor of a quick solution is the lack of adjustments made to sustain the changes made. What makes sense in the moment might not be sustainable long-term, or it might create greater friction and more problems than it solves elsewhere.

The last trade-off is desirability. "How disruptive will this be?" Will your people like it? Will your sales team use it? A great solution that's not utilized does no one any good.

TIPS AND TAKEAWAYS

In Chapter 9, we covered the first element of structure: system design. When creating your system design, it is important to:

- Maximize value creation by treating the four steps of system design as an ongoing process,
- Define and differentiate between your complicated and complex problems,
- And manage friction tax to reduce complexity and increase the effortlessness of growth.

System design is the process of managing trade-offs and adjustments that are necessary to align all inputs toward your objective. It is an ongoing process that maximizes value creation, manages friction, and minimizes needless complexity as the first element of structure which leads to greater growth for your business.

CHAPTER 10

THE TECH STACK

MANY YEARS AGO, WHEN I WAS PLAYING GOLF ON A SEMI-REGULAR basis, I got to a point where I was really struggling with upping my game. So, I went out and bought a new set of clubs. Right after I bought those clubs, there was an immediate (though, in all candor, slight) improvement in my game. That improvement didn't stick. Pretty soon, I had reverted back to my same old struggle with golf. The shiny new clubs didn't fix anything.

The common adage is that the clubs don't make the golfer. But I'd add a caveat to that. If you want to improve just your next round of golf, go ahead and buy that new set of clubs. Your next round of golf is likely going to be better because you have new clubs. You have new tools. And that sense of novelty will make you that much more attentive to the game. You're going to be more focused. You're going to be more excited to play...for all of one round, unfortunately.

The improvement from new tools is temporary if you don't also fix the underlying system, which is the golfer in this example. When nothing fundamentally changes, new tools don't enable a better solution. The same is true when you're looking at your tools in business.

In today's age, when you're talking about tools, you're talking about tech.

The tools you use, your tech, is the second component of structure. Your tech stack and tools will not be the reason you win. However, your tech stack is still important to integrate into the structure you build, so we are still going to discuss the five main principles and components of an effective tech stack.

THE FIVE PRINCIPLES FOR IMPLEMENTING AN EFFECTIVE TECH STACK

1. The business process must drive the technology, not the other way around.
2. The simplest stack that meets the organization or system's needs is the best tech stack.
3. Automation is the byproduct of a good process, not the objective. If you can't do it manually, you can't automate it.
4. Don't buy technology; hire it. Focus on the Jobs to Be Done.
5. Solve for the whole (the business).

DON'T BUY TECHNOLOGY

Don't buy technology. Hire it.

When considering adding technology, any technology, don't pay attention to the features; focus on defining the job that needs to be done, and the problem that needs to be solved. Never forget that technology, despite what the providers say, is not a solution. At best it's an enabler or an accelerator for a solution.

Here's a simple way to define the job/problem. Just answer these four questions:

What is the outcome that you desire?

What is the gap?

What are the symptoms or indicators?

Then, dig into the causes. **Is it a people problem, a process problem,**

or a tech problem? It might even be a combination of the three, but you can't get into it without having addressed the first three questions. I've talked to and advised sales tech companies who count on the fact that you're not doing the first three steps. They're depending on your inability to define the problem in order to sell you tech as the solution.

Another component to "hiring" the right tech for the Jobs to Be Done is doing regular performance reviews. When assessing the application of new (or existing) tech stacks, keep the following questions in mind:

- What did we hire this application for?
- What's changed since we hired it? How is it performing?
- What else is out there?
- Can we reduce the headcount by combining apps?
- Can this job be done by something else in our text app?
- How is this application getting along with the others?

At the end of the day, your decision to *not* utilize a tech application can also be a use of tech. No tech is still utilizing tech in the same way that inaction is also an action.

TOY OR TOOL?

The most damaging emotion that every tech provider today takes advantage of is the "fear of missing out," or FOMO. So much technology is built up by stories of how the specific tech has made someone's life so very easy, and you'd have to be a fool to not buy it...right now. The thing is, FOMO matters for toys. It doesn't matter for tools. Your tech stack plays a key role in ensuring that you have the insights to make great decisions so you can execute powerfully. The way you choose to implement the tech as a core element of your system design will have far more influence on the behaviors of your salespeople than any strategic retreat, compensation, or bonus plan will ever have.

Another pitfall that costs companies more money than you can even begin to imagine is the belief that technology is the solution. If you remember nothing else from this chapter, maybe even nothing else from this book, please remember this:

Technology is not the solution.

A company's growth efforts are only as strong as the decisions they make and the platform that they have to execute those decisions. At best, a great tech stack is an accelerator or an enabler for your system to reach its solutions. So, don't buy technology to solve a problem. Buy technology to enable the solution that's been designed in your systems and structure.

NO TECHNOLOGY IS TECHNOLOGY

To be clear, when I talk about building tech stacks, I'm not just talking about gaining tech.

One of the common beliefs that developed in recent years, especially because we've become such a technology-dominated society, is you have to add technology in order to improve a tech stack. And the reality is that not having an application doesn't mean you don't have technology. If you're using pencil and paper...well, a pencil is actually technology too.

So don't fall into the trap of thinking, "If there's an app for it, I need it. Because technology!" That's putting you right back into the toy trap. When it comes to building effective tech stacks, it's okay to not have every bucket filled.

EIGHTY-BILLION-DOLLAR WHITE ELEPHANT

Let's also talk about your core tech platform—the CRM.

CRM is the biggest white elephant in the history of tech. It's estimated that companies spend 4.6 billion annually on CRM implementations. Today, CRM represents the largest category in the business tech stack with an anticipated $80 billion of annual revenue by 2025. But despite its prevalence, something is still fundamentally wrong with the implementation of most CRMs.

Over the last two years, I've been involved in more than a hundred implementations across 30 different industries, working with sales organizations ranging from as small as 3 to as big as 350. Depending on what research or study you use, technology implementations (especially for core apps like CRM) fail to deliver on their intended results 50 to 70 percent of the time. Why? It's primarily due to poor adoption and poor utilization. There are also three core contributors that contribute to poor adoption and poor utilization.

Number one, when you're implementing a CRM, small misalignments are magnified. Ideally, we buy a piece of technology that enables our system design to solve friction. But if we haven't thought through all of the elements that have led to the friction, all those small things get magnified. Technology is an accelerator. It can accelerate solutions, but it can also accelerate problems.

Number two, inertia is a powerful beast (and we've all got day jobs). When you are changing your tech stack, you affect system design, which affects structure. Structure guides behavior, so when you change technology, you are changing behavior at some point down the line. Remember it is the changed behavior that causes new results, not just acquiring a new tech or tool. Inevitably, I see companies regularly try to change too much, too fast, without having a solid system design to reduce the friction of execution for their salespeople. Inevitably, when salespeople operate under the stress of inadequately supported change, adoption becomes a major barrier. Those companies never even get to the point of utilization.

Number three, there's a difference between the theory and the reality of how things work. When you're designing systems, you get to do it in a laboratory. But in the real world, things don't work like they do in perfectly controlled or purely hypothetical environments. So, a lot of people tend to overcompensate and over-design, and over-apply tech. This results in a system that is quite rigid and lacks resilience. Such a system will break down at the first sign of a real-world problem.

In the world of business growth, sales, marketing, revenue acquisition, and revenue expansion, everything is always changing. If your system is not built to iterate, then it will not deliver on results.

TIPS AND TAKEAWAYS

In Chapter 10, we covered the second element of structure: tech stacks. When selecting the appropriate tech tools for your business, you should be mindful of:

- The five principles for an effective tech stack,
- The common fallacy of treating tech as a solution or toy,
- And the Jobs to Be Done by hiring (rather than buying) tech.

When we talk about tools in business, we're often talking about tech. Although your tech stack will never be the first element of structure (it will *not* be the reason you win), a careful and conscious choice of tech tools will be the reason you don't lose your game in business...which leads us to the third element of an effective structure—the scoreboard.

CHAPTER 11

THE SCOREBOARD

WHAT IS THE PROFESSION BEST SUITED FOR A LIAR?

For years, one of the top responses to that question has been "sales." The other popular responses are usually "lawyer" or "politician," and for those of you who've worked in marketing over the last decade, you're not low on the list either. Jokes about dishonest salespeople are as common as punchlines about airplane food.

How do you know when a salesperson is lying? Their lips are moving. What's the difference between a used car salesperson and a SaaS salesperson? At least the used car salesperson knows they're lying. (Don't forget to tip your bartenders.)

Pretend for a moment that you're an executive having to deal with these salespeople. You come into work knowing that you've got a crazy schedule ahead of you. You sit down at your desk, already wondering how you're going to surf the tide of the week's appointments. You look at your calendar for the day and see a 1:30 p.m. meeting with a salesperson. What are you feeling at that moment? If you're like most people, you can feel your blood pressure rising, and you're thinking of some choice words that would have to be censored in this book. Under your breath, you might ask, "Why the hell did I schedule this meeting today? How do I get out of this?"

Sales has a horrible reputation. But for the vast majority of salespeople, this reputation is undeserved. For every joke poking fun at the archetypical "pushy salesman," there are dozens of encounters that people have with pleasant and empathetic salespeople, salespeople that they think of very fondly as important connections within the industry. Yet, instead of calling them salespeople, the buyers will call them a "trusted advisor," or "consultant." It's as if buyers don't want to outright say they get along with "salespeople." But if sales was as bad as its reputations, there's no way any commerce would be generated. Markets would completely crash, and businesses would burn. So, why all the hate?

Most of the negative perception stems from the misconception that salespeople are motivated by one thing and one thing only: commissions. For the most part, salespeople today have a portion of their compensation based on commissions; it all comes down to whether or not they make the sale. I think it's important to note the complete fallacy of this belief. As an entrepreneur and owner of a small business, my entire livelihood is also based on making sales. Yet, entrepreneurs and business owners by and large don't suffer the same negative perception of being commission-oriented or pushy. Why is that?

The truth is, salespeople aren't actually motivated by commission. Studies, such as those discussed in the books by Daniel Pink, author of *Drive*, have proven that salespeople are not motivated by money more than anybody else.

If salespeople aren't motivated by money, then what are they motivated by? The same things as everybody else—winning. More on this later in the chapter.

For now, let's overcome the tendency to see salespeople as pushy jerks. Instead, let's look at the underlying cause that leads to these negative perceptions around salespeople and creates myriad other challenges for a growth-focused business.

KPI AND KEY METRICS

GOODHART'S LAW (DATA AND THE EXPERIENCE FALLACY)

As much as I love data, the business world has become obsessed—too obsessed—with it. There's an addiction to numbers and metrics. Unfortunately, that obsession is distracting, and data for most businesses is more like a lamppost for a drunk, used for support rather than illumination. Under the auspices of being smart, being scientific, or being purposeful, we throw data and metrics around. We build dashboards that are more all-encompassing than anything I've ever seen before.

The problem isn't the data or the metrics themselves. It's how people use them. Data became in vogue in the first place because smart people used data, metrics, and analytics as a tool for thinking. Then, everybody else looked at the smart guys and thought, "Oh, it's about data. Okay, that's what we should focus on." And then a bunch of organizations ended up replacing actual thought with data.

Much like with tech, too many companies mistakenly expect data to be their answer rather than a tool to help them ask better questions and enable them to find solutions. This mistake is so prevalent in business; there's even a law to go along with it—Goodhart's Law. "When a measure becomes a target, it ceases to be a good measure."

> Hey, this email performed really well!
>
> What made it perform so well?
>
> Uh, it had a 10 percent click rate.
>
> Oh, so we want a 10 percent click rate!

So, there's the problem. An email isn't successful because it has a 10 percent click rate. It has a 10 percent click rate because it is successful. When we look to data for answers and replace thinking with counting, we turn a reasonable measure like click rate into a target. We let metrics replace the role of management and decision-making.

The mistakes don't stop there. We humans, even the most conscientious of us, are subject to what's called the "experience fallacy." Everyone has an opinion when it comes to what works in sales, marketing, or customer success, because everyone's got some experience. We've either done it ourselves or been on the buyer's side of it. While these opinions can be important, they're just opinions. They're not facts.

You see, the fundamental problem with opinions is that they're based almost exclusively on the experiences and prejudices of the person who holds said opinions. In a world like sales or marketing, where things are always changing, You can't sustain the use of data and metrics without the right approach. Unfortunately, some people are inclined to take the wrong approach because of the experience fallacy. They overweigh the validity of what they perceive to be true rather than using the data to dig deeper and enable better questions to be asked.

While I definitely do not think data can tell the entire story, I do think data can tell a compelling component of the story when used properly, when we push back against our experience fallacy.

LAGGING AND LEADING INDICATORS

How do we use data to identify areas that we can influence and change?

The only valuable analytic if you're in a growth motion is the one that gives you the ability to form an intervention. Don't tell me that we're going to finish 20 percent below expectations. Tell me that we're in danger of being 20 percent below expectations, and give me insights on things that I can do to change. Because if the data is only telling me what's true without telling me what I can do, it's not creating any meaningful value.

To utilize data effectively, we need to separate and understand the difference between a lagging metric and a leading metric. Profit, sales, and revenue are lagging metrics. They tell us what has happened. These lagging indicators are important to understanding past performances, but they don't provide meaningful guidance for future growth.

A leading indicator is a signal or a metric that looks forward. It is designed to increase predictability of future outcomes and events. A lagging indicator looks backward, and its purpose is to provide insight or a signal as to whether the intended result was achieved or not.

An example of a leading indicator is a metric we use called "meaningful conversations." A meaningful conversation is a conversation where (1) we learn at least one piece of material information that enables us to personalize, contextualize, and/or customer our approach to the prospect, and (2) both parties (salesperson and prospect) commit to taking a definable action by a specific time. I know that the more meaningful conversations a salesperson has, the more opportunities they'll create and ultimately the more they will win. I'm also able to identify a target meaningful conversation range so that if a sales rep drops below a certain level we can make adjustments before their results deteriorate.

WHAT YOU MEASURE MATTERS, BUT HOW YOU MEASURE IS CRITICAL

Here's another example of a (very) common mistake that's made when measuring. One of the most common key metrics and leading indicators that growth executives use is pipeline capture, or what I refer to as "win rate."

Win rate calculates the percentage of deals a company will win, based on the total number of deals they create. This metric is important for many reasons, not the least of which is that you need to know how much potential business you need in your pipeline to be confident that you'll be able to achieve your revenue and growth targets.

This calculation leads to another common metric called "pipeline coverage." Pipeline coverage is the total revenue potential of all open deals that are needed to be confident that you will be able to achieve your target revenue goal. If your pipeline coverage equals 3x, that means that if your revenue target is $1 million, you need $3 million in your pipeline. The most common multiples fall in the 3 to 5x range.

You may be asking how the multiple is determined. For most people, they take the inverse of their closing or win rates. So if your rate is 20 percent that equates to a 5x multiple, while a 33 percent rate equates to a 3x multiple.

Here's where it gets interesting. How do most companies calculate their close/win rates? While this may seem like a very simple question, your answer is going to have a big impact. If you're like most, you'll take the number of opportunities you win and divide that by the number of opportunities that are created.

If you create 20 opportunities and with eight of those, your win rate equals 40 percent. Seems simple enough.

Did you catch the conflict? Take a moment and consider what's wrong with that approach.

The example above (eight opportunities won from 20 created) calculates what I call your n-factor win rate, or the win rate for the number of opportunities. But, if you're trying to calculate your pipeline coverage multiple, the important metric isn't the n-factor win rate; it's the dollar-weighted win rate, and very rarely are the two the same.

In our experience, unless there is a clear structure in place, the n-factor win rate is typically 2 to 4 times greater than the $-weighted win rate. Look at this example below (taken from a real win-rate analysis we did for a client of ours).

Success Rate Deal Count

	Total	Wins	Losses	In Progress	Win %	Loss %	IP %
Sales Rep 1	80	30	21	37	34.09%	23.86%	42.05%
Sales Rep 2	59	21	14	24	35.59%	23.73%	40.68%
Sales Rep 3	126	59	12	55	46.83%	9.52%	43.65%
Sales Rep 4	170	60	12	98	35.29%	7.06%	57.65%
Sales Rep 5	71	26	22	23	36.62%	30.99%	32.39%
Sales Rep 6	81	25	39	17	30.86%	48.15%	20.99%
Sales Rep 7	33	20	2	11	60.61%	6.06%	33.33%
Sales Rep 8	93	33	37	23	35.48%	39.78%	24.73%
Totals	721	274	159	288	38.00%	22.05%	39.94%
Average per rep	90.13	34.25	19.88	36.00			

Success Rate Revenue

	Total	Wins	Losses	In Progress	Win %	Loss %	IP %
Sales Rep 1	$ 9,629,931	$ 261,435	$ 805,236	$ 8,552,100	2.71%	8.36%	88.81%
Sales Rep 2	$ 1,449,166	$ 384,610	$ 328,474	$ 685,219	26.54%	22.67%	47.28%
Sales Rep 3	$ 12,360,051	$ 2,195,125	$ 899,906	$ 9,166,205	17.76%	7.28%	74.16%
Sales Rep 4	$ 3,303,188	$ 587,134	$ 532,615	$ 2,163,920	17.77%	16.12%	65.51%
Sales Rep 5	$ 3,239,038	$ 608,102	$ 442,191	$ 2,301,281	18.77%	13.65%	71.05%
Sales Rep 6	$ 8,260,916	$ 744,748	$ 5,346,351	$ 2,190,089	9.02%	64.72%	26.51%
Sales Rep 7	$ 752,101	$ 202,237	$ 21,421	$ 526,903	26.89%	2.85%	70.06%
Sales Rep 8	$ 31,523,529	$ 2,002,936	$ 27,883,780	$ 1,770,873	6.35%	88.45%	5.62%
Totals	$ 70,571,916	$ 6,986,326	$ 36,259,974	$ 27,356,590	9.1%	51.42%	38.79%
Average per rep	$ 8,814,739	$ 873,291	$ 4,532,497	$ 3,419,574			

Deal Count vs. Revenue

	Wins	Losses	IP %
Deal Count	38.00%	22.05%	39.94%
Revenue	9.91%	51.41%	38.79%

The company in this example used a pipeline coverage multiple of 2.5 to manage their projections and forecasting. This makes sense given the win rate they tracked typically hovered around 40 percent. One of the reasons we were brought in to work with this company was because of the disruption their growth efforts were causing them. When we shared this analysis with them and they realized that they were regularly winning less than 10 percent of the dollar value of their combined pipeline, things became very clear for them.

Changing how they measured things impacted several initiatives and led to a clearer path to achieve their targeted outcomes.

LET'S TALK QUOTAS

The most common "scoreboard" in sales is the sales quota. Sales (or revenue) quotas are a foundational element for sales. Yet, for most people, the only question about quotas that is ever asked is, "What should the target revenue or customer acquisition success quota be set at?" Questioning the need, appropriateness, or effectiveness of the target itself is sacrilegious in most business circles.

But I don't quota my reps on revenue, because revenue quotas are lagging indicators that measure results. They don't measure causes or contributors.

In 2010, the Texas Rangers beat the New York Yankees to get into the World Series. What struck me was just how well they took advantage of their opportunities. The opportunistic nature was no accident. Their hitting coach, Clint Hurdle, believed in a concept he calls "Positive Plate Appearances" (also called productive at-bats). According to Hurdle, there are eight ways you can have a positive at-bat:

- Hit
- Walk
- Sac bunt
- Sac fly
- HBP/Catcher's Interference
- Move lead runner up w/an out
- Move lead runner up w/an error
- 8 pitch AB

Most people only think of the first two as productive, but Hurdle understood—and was able to get his players to understand—that it takes many things to score a run. By focusing on "advancing" the opportunity to score a run rather than on scoring, the probability of scoring increases. The Texas Rangers set a goal of 17 Positive Plate Appearances per game. No surprise that the Rangers led the league in that category.

The same approach applies to selling. Sales quotes put all of the focus on the result. Just like in baseball where a hitter can do everything right and hit into a double play or do a bunch of things wrong and end up with an off-the-end-of-the-bat double, a salesperson can do everything right and still lose the sale. When quota is the "scoreboard," you get the types of behaviors that have led sales to get their negative stereotypes.

Here's how I approach this in my company. When I did an analysis of my own organization, I found that in a typical month somewhere between 2 and 5 percent of companies in our target market were going to experience a behavior-changing event. This event would be important enough and critical enough that they were going to reach outside of their organization. It might be research. It might be seeking opinions. It might be looking for a specific solution to help address a problem or incoming opportunity.

It became clear to me that the single best thing I could do for my organization, the single best thing that any salesperson could do, is generate relevant relationships with companies that fit our organization's profile. If the company had a question, if they needed to get an answer to something or get someone's opinion, would they reach out to us to ask that question? If the answer was yes, then we had a relevant relationship.

Once I'd determined the scoreboard we actually needed to track in order to win, I set about changing that scoring system for my sales team. I said to my reps, "I want you to develop 200 relationships."

I wanted sales to develop relationships with growth organizations where we were relevant. If 2 to 5 percent of those 200 companies had a new question or new problem that month, it meant that 4 to 10 companies would reach out to my sales reps to ask them a question. Somewhere between a third or a half of those companies that reached out to us would have an issue that justified a deeper dive into their operations, and that became a sales opportunity.

I did not (and could not) create the need for change; I simply knew it would inevitably happen. The best thing I and my sales team could do was be relevant and be on the buyer's mind when that change happened. This would begin what I will refer to as a "meaningful conversation" with the client company.

The "meaningful conversation" is a conversation where the sales rep learns something material about a potential customer that would enable us to personalize, contextualize, and customize our approach. Within a meaningful conversation, both parties would agree to and commit to doing something with specificity by a certain time, and this increased the likelihood of enabling a successful outcome for our customers.

Our reps quota focuses on meaningful conversations. Meaningful conversations determined what their comp rate was on the business that they closed. By changing the quota, we incentivized a winning behavior in our reps. We generated more opportunities. Even with the reduced pressure, our average sales size increased. Simultaneously, the average time for each sale decreased.

With that change in the scoreboard and resulting change in behavior, our new business saw growth to the tune of 75 percent within a period of 18 months. We saw similar success after correcting the scoreboard for the companies we worked with.

The most instantaneous and amazing difference was the change within sales. When I changed the quota, I changed the behavioral incentives for my sales team. The scoreboard, and consequently the structure, of winning stopped being about the quantity of business that was closed. It started being about how many meaningful conversations we had, and how many companies we could foster strong relevant relationships with.

When I ask an organization, "Are you winning? How do you know?", I'm looking for evidence of a solid structure for great behavioral change. The organizations that are able to point to the scoreboard, tech stacks, and system design which build that structure are the organizations that will ultimately win.

ARE YOU WINNING?

Whenever I'm brought in to assess an organization, its structure, or its system design, one of my two favorite questions to ask is, "Are you winning?" And if the response is, "Heck yeah. We're winning!" The follow-up question I like to ask is, "How do you know?" How do you know, at the end of the day or week or month or quarter… How do you know if you're winning or not? From what I've seen, the best organizations are the ones that have the most people who can answer that question clearly. And the answers they give aren't typically the answers that we think matter.

If you ask a salesperson if they're having a good month, and they only give you their sales number, that's not a particularly good sign. In poker, they call that resulting—judging the quality of the actions that you take by the result of those actions. When determining your scoreboard, you want to avoid resulting. In a complex system, the only thing we can control is what we put into the system and how we manage things when they happen.

In sales and in marketing, we can do the right things and lose a sale; we can do the wrong things and win. So, instead of judging right or wrong actions by the best or worst outcomes, we must aim for the best opportunities to sustain a winning performance.

TIPS AND TAKEAWAYS

In Chapter 11, we covered the third element of structure: the scoreboard. When building and tracking your scoreboard, it is important to:

- Treat data as a tool to ask better questions,
- Analyze the scoreboard without letting metrics replace conscious decision-making,
- And choose the right quota that incentivizes winning behavior.

When you guide the people in your organization by building an effective structure according to the three elements of system design, tech stacks, and scoreboard, you can enable consistent action from your salespeople toward greater opportunities and increase your business's probability of achieving its RevOps and growth objectives.

PART IV

APPROACH

CHAPTER 12

APPROACH OVERVIEW

EARLY IN 2004, A FRIEND OF AN ASSOCIATE OF MINE REACHED OUT to me after I'd started my company, Imagine. At the time, Imagine was a sales advisory company, and this friend of an associate had a team of 12 salespeople he wanted advice for. For Imagine, it was the ideal opportunity.

His team was already doing well, but there was some frustration still. He felt like they could be doing much better. Not only did he feel it, but he was also convinced of it. I remember him telling me, "We're doing okay, but we *should* be doing much better."

Having heard great things about my unique approach to sales and sales organizations, he wanted us to advise him and implement a sales coaching program for his team so they could become better salespeople.

So, as with most implementations, we began with an assessment. I came in and looked over his overall go-to-market strategy, his messaging—fundamental things like that. I looked at what he was doing for his company website. I interviewed several of the salespeople in his team. I looked at all the data that I'd accumulated while I was there. Finally, the time had come to share with him what my findings were.

"You don't have a sales problem."

"Well, what do you mean by that?" he asked.

I explained to him, "What you *want* to have is a sales problem, but that isn't the real problem you're facing right now. As a matter of fact, if I were to train your salespeople, if we were to adjust the sales structure and do all the things that we've talked about that sound like they would be good solutions for sales, it would probably do you more harm than good."

He gave me a confused look and said, "I don't see how helping my salespeople be better can hurt me."

And I said, "Well, even if your sales team gets better at initiating conversations and approaching things from a customer-centric perspective, it wouldn't do any good when potential customers leave those conversations and visit your website, where your messaging is all over the place."

"So the real problem is the messaging?"

"It's more than that." I explained, "You're lacking a cohesive approach. So while we could work with your sales team to change their game, every action that we'd be taking would be contradicted by other elements of your approach."

His current barrier wasn't upleveling the skills of his salespeople, he needed to adjust and align his go-to-market strategy. The time would come when an investment in his salespeople would be the right thing to do, but they needed to address other areas first. He needed to figure out his strategy, what differentiated him from competitors, and what game he was trying to win. What he needed was a shift in mindset.

THE RIGHT MINDSET TO APPROACH BUSINESS

If you haven't been able to tell by how many times I've said it by now, I've always been into business. I grew up in an entrepreneurial family, and I've always been a student of business. I've been fascinated by the decisions, the actions, the adjustments, and the results that businesses achieve.

I read somewhere that less than 1 percent of people who attend college expect to end up in sales when they graduate. I was one of those 1 percent. I always knew that I was going to go into sales because that was the best way for me to be able to start a business. To run my own business successfully, I had to master the art of selling.

And from the time I first got into business, I heard a phrase that I've paraphrased many times since, but never really understood until a few years ago. That phrase is:

Work on your business, not in your business.

It's a phrase that sounds motivational, yet I always found it very difficult to embrace in my early career. Why? Well, as someone who was used to running small businesses, I was, in many ways, staying at the center of what my businesses were doing. Sure, I'd love to work on my business, but if I'm working *on* the business, who's going to work *in* the business?

After reflecting on the decades of work I've done with mid-market companies, here's what I've come to learn. That catchphrase predominantly came from consultants and speakers who succeeded in large businesses. And there's no doubt the fundamental advantage that the largest companies have over smaller and mid-market companies is the resources and people available to them. The largest businesses can afford to work on initiatives rather than exclusively delivering and executing on a day-to-day basis. Smaller businesses simply can't.

It took me several years of trial and error to finally understand how to apply "working *on* your business" in a world where resources aren't sufficient to fully specialize between the strategic elements of working on the business and the tactical elements of working in the business.

For smaller and mid-market companies, the first step to working *on* business comes down to identifying a clear approach.

FINDING YOUR MO

Every company, every organization, every person, whether they really realize it or not, has an MO—a modus operandi. (A "je ne sais quoi," if you will.) The problem is, for most people, their own MO is invisible. There's a way they do something, but that "way" isn't clear to them. The people they work with aren't completely clear, and their prospects and customers aren't clear either. With each iteration, things are always a little bit different. That works fine when you're just starting out and when your business is small.

But as you grow, you manage more complexity. As more people are involved, your failure to have a defined, purposeful MO will create confusion and prevent your business from doing the single most important thing a business can do: learn.

The transformation from a people- or behavioral-driven organization to a structure- and process-driven one requires an identifiable and well-defined approach. This is crucial if you want to be able to sustain growth, let alone scale. This doesn't mean that people aren't important in a structure or process-driven organization. The real reason why approach is so crucial is not because it can replace people, but because the only way you can manage the complexity of growth and diversity, both internal and external, is to create alignment for your people and your structure. A unifying alignment requires a clear and conscious approach.

In most organizations, whether the people in that organization realize it or not, everybody is doing the best they can. Everybody in there is making the best decisions in the best way to try to achieve the best outcomes for themselves and their organization. But without a clear approach, there's no way for people to know if they're all pulling in the same direction.

Imagine your company was a big rock surrounded by ten people, a hundred people, or even ten thousand people, and each person is pulling as hard as they can on their own rope that's tied around the rock. If everybody is pulling as hard as they can in every direction, that rock won't budge. Without proper alignment of effort, an organization has no velocity.

Your approach—your process, methodology, and playbooks—creates the constructs and the constraints you use to align your people's efforts into momentum and velocity for your organization.

TIPS AND TAKEAWAYS

In Chapter 12, we discussed the importance of having a cohesive approach to business. A cohesive and clear approach would:

- Allow you to work on your business as well as in your business,
- Help manage the complexity of growth and diversity as a manifestation of your structure,
- And create a unifying alignment for your people that turns their efforts into greater velocity toward your business's objectives.

While the structure of your business is the invisible hand, the manifestation of that structure is your approach—your modus operandi. It is a combination of your processes, your methodologies, and your playbooks—the key components of approach, which we will explore in the following chapters.

CHAPTER 13

PROCESS

JOE MADDEN, THE MANAGER WHO LED THE CHICAGO CUBS TO their first World Series win since 1908, professed during an interview that "our goal on a day-to-day basis is not to win games."

Imagine that for a moment. Joe Madden, the manager of a major league baseball team, the manager in a sport where the purpose is to win games so the team can go to the playoffs and win more games with the hopes of ultimately winning the World Series, the manager who is arguably one of the best, most successful managers in history, said that the goal is not to win games.

In the same interview, he goes on to say, "It [our goal] is on executing our game plan and process."

Madden believes (and I'd have to agree) that bad things happen when the focus is on the result of what you do, rather than on the effective execution of what you set out to do. You show me an athlete, an organization, or a performer that is consistently successful, and I will show you someone who has defined a clear process for themselves and who stays focused on the process.

Of course, the challenge comes when you can't focus on the process because you lack a clear, conscious understanding of what your process is.

THREE REASONS WHY PROCESS FAILS

If processes are important to results, then why are so many people skeptical about the effectiveness of a clear, defined process? Why do processes fail?

One of the main reasons why processes tend to fail is because they're too rigid. This is one of the first mistakes most people make when they define their process. They get really, really excited about it. They see the potential of a process that creates clarity...so they make a 100-step process, detailing everything. I have literally had a CEO show me their 127-step process for how they win a customer. I'm not kidding; it was really 127 steps! It was beautifully written and planned out with painstaking precision. And it was never going to work because it was too rigid. With 127 steps, this process was so specific that it had no resilience or flexibility. In the face of real-world problems, which all have a degree of unpredictability and chaos, this 127-step process broke down and became useless. As a result, the rigid process failed.

This is in contrast to the second major problem of ineffective processes, which is being too vague. I've seen processes where the "steps" were more like abstract, philosophical statements. There were no concrete, tangible steps to these processes. They were so vague that they didn't create any constraint which could be used for alignment within an organization. As a result, these vague processes failed.

Both of these situations are caused by the human tendency to view processes from a bottom-up perspective, rather than a top-down perspective. When I talk about top-down or bottom-up, I'm referring to the top point as strategy and the bottom point as execution. "Top-down" starts from the strategy and works down toward the point of execution. In contrast, "bottom-up" starts at the point of execution and makes sense of it by working upward.

When I landed my first professional sales job in 1989, during my first sales training, I was taught that the most important scale to measure was closing. To this day, the world of sales is dealing with the myth that closing is the most important element of the sale. That's why plays like *Glengarry Glen Ross* create famous lines like, "Coffee is for closers." That's why the salespeople who are involved at the end of the sales process tend to get paid the most. It's all built on this misconception that closing is the most important part of the process.

Well, why do people believe that closing is the most important? In a sales interaction, closing is what happens right before someone says yes or no. To some degree, we've all experienced recency bias, where we think the cause happens just before the consequence.

It wasn't until Neil Rackham came along and shared his research in his seminal book, *SPIN Selling*, that the evidence against the contrary really became more known. As demonstrated through Rackham's research, closing was not only *not* the most important part of the process, but it was actually far less important than most other elements. Sales weren't won because of what happened in the closing. They were won (or lost) much earlier in the process. The results manifested themselves today, while they were earned yesterday.

If you had to map out a decision tree where you had to make ten choices, though each choice only had two options, you'd end up with 1,024 different outcomes at the bottom. Bottom-up process design is overwhelming, and that's the third main reason processes fail; you're looking at things bottom-up instead of top-down. You're dealing with symptoms rather than solutions. It's a hornet's nest.

When we're designing sales processes for companies, I like to ask, "What does a typical sale look like?" And the most common answer is, "Well, it's always different."

If you're looking at the 1,024 different outcomes from the bottom, then yes, you're right. A typical sale seems anything but typical each time. However, to reach any of those 1,024 outcomes, you never had to make a choice between more than two options at a time. So, from the top-down, it was actually a very simple, very standard process.

In my experience, the true drivers of outcomes are determined within the first levels of a process matrix, or decision tree. When you're doing a bottom-up analysis, you're starting off with complexity, and that's the wrong end of the process to be.

Remember Gall's Law: complexity builds from simplicity. If you start off at the complicated end, you'll never be able to make sense of anything. The key is to start at the top and work your way down, to solve downstream problems from upstream.

MAP YOUR PROCESS FROM INTEREST TO REVENUE

Although there may be more than one process that succeeds, the ones that are designed too rigid, too vague, or from the bottom-up perspective rarely become part of an effective approach. So, the best thing that you can do to create clarity and consistency within an environment of chaos, anarchy, and confusion is to map out the process. You can start by mapping your customer acquisition process from interest to revenue.

At Imagine, we've reviewed thousands of full-cycle sales interactions. We've advised, debriefed, discussed, and interviewed hundreds of sellers and buyers. We've often had the opportunity after a seller and buyer meet to interview the two about their interaction. We've asked them what they expected to happen and what actually happened. And we've reviewed reams of data, metrics, and analytics to identify what's really happening in the customer journey, from the point where a potential buyer's not thinking about doing anything to one day writing a million-dollar check and changing the direction of their entire organization.

Long before I developed the Revenue Acceleration Framework, from the time I was about seven years old, I've been fascinated by one single question: Why do people do what they do?

What drew me to the world of sales was my need to understand why people make the decisions that they make when risk is involved. To a large degree, this fascination was the driving factor for my years of research into the buyer's journey. And at Imagine, what we've learned is that the commonly used models that define the buyer's journey are wrong.

When you dig into it, "buying" is not a singular activity. Buying is the combined process of learning and deciding.

So much of what we've been taught in sales and marketing is inaccurate on a fundamental level. We've been taught that the buyer's journey is a very linear, logical model. We've been taught that it operates like a series of gates. In reality, it's more like a pinball machine. Better yet, I'd say making a sale is like making a snowball in that pinball machine. As it bounces off of pins, the snowball picks up more and more snow, gaining mass.

AN INSIGHT INTO INDECISION

Unfortunately, people hate making decisions, and there is a good reason why. Deciding is a very strenuous human activity.

My favorite behavioral psychology trivia is: Did you know that the word "homicide" and the word "decide" have the same Latin root and mean the same thing? They both mean to kill. When you decide, you are killing other options. Think about what happens in most homes sometime in the evening. The question gets asked, "What do you want for dinner?" If you're like my family, 90 minutes later we're throwing something in the microwave because no one has made a decision. Now, imagine if the decision really mattered.

When asked to make decisions, people hooked up to brain MRIs and skin response tests triggered the same biological responses people experience when they perceive they're in danger. Indecision is like a manifestation of the fight, flight, or freeze fear response.

There's a common belief, especially in sales and marketing, that people don't like to say yes. So, reps create all kinds of creative (sometimes manipulative) ways to work around that tendency of human behavior. But that belief misses half of the equation: People don't like to say yes, but they don't like to say no either.

When it comes to closing, our job is not about managing a sale. It's about managing a decision.

In order for more people to make decisions, we need to enable them to feel safe when making decisions. And to make people feel safe when they're making decisions, we need to understand how people learn.

Luckily for us, there is a tremendous amount of very good research that highlights the process that people go through when they're learning.

One of my favorite learning models, which I got from *The Design of Business* by Roger Martin, is something called the "knowledge funnel."

Right at the top of the funnel is the mystery stage where everything is unknown. Everything is a guess. As someone learns and gains experience, heuristics emerge. This is the key to the learning process:

Humans live on heuristics.

Heuristics are general themes that, in a person's (perceived) experience, are true far more often than they're not. Heuristics match the patterns that align with the beliefs we carry, and those confirmed beliefs guide the decisions we make. Our job in the beginning is to help people navigate the mystery stage of that funnel and support or influence their heuristics. By having a role in the learning and decision processes and making potential customers comfortable with saying yes or no, we defeat indecision.

THE 5 STAGES OF THE BUYER'S JOURNEY

When it comes to understanding the buyer's journey, there are five general stages of the processes that you'll need to map out for your business.

Remember, as we cover each part of the buyer's journey, to think about what steps your business takes to fulfill each stage. The power of mapping the process is mapping the hypothesis of what you think is happening. With that hypothesis clear, you and your team will more quickly determine what points on your map were correct and what points were off. Having that hypothesis will accelerate your learning cycles and increase momentum, making it much easier to define an effective process for your approach.

FIRST STAGE: EPIPHANY

You can also think of this as the pre-epiphany stage. This is where your potential customer isn't thinking about what you do one way or the other. They are not paying any attention. They are not thinking about it. In the vast majority of markets, somewhere between 90 and 95 percent of people are either not thinking about the issue that you address, or they think they're happy with what they already have.

In the previous chapter, I mentioned the conscious mind likes to think of itself as the Oval Office when it's actually the press office. That aspect of human psychology is the basis for the epiphany phase. When it comes to generating business opportunities, humans are far more open to influence when we're not thinking about something. The epiphany phase is your greatest opportunity to influence how people start to think about the issues that you address.

Furthermore, if you want people to think differently about who they're buying from, get them to think differently about the issue that they're trying to solve. You've achieved the epiphany phase when you hit what I like to call the "oh, shit" moment. Nobody ever does things differently without first reaching an "oh, shit" moment. One of the truisms that I've followed for years is: "Whoever controls the 'oh, shit' moment controls the market."

Susan Scott, author of *Fierce Conversations* and *Achieving Success at Work & in Life*, popularized the phrase, "the problem named is the problem solved." The epiphany is when the problem is named.

When naming problems, it's useful to remember that there are commonly two types of problems. Bad problems and good problems. I sometimes call them trouble problems and opportunity problems, but regardless of terminology, it all comes back to the problem that's named is the problem that's solved.

The number one reason why the people who should be buying from you are not buying from you is that they've named their problem incorrectly for you. There is a level of disconnect there. They haven't had their "oh, shit" moment. Influence how buyers define their problem, and you'll change how they behave.

SECOND STAGE: ENGAGEMENT

Once a potential customer starts thinking, "Oh shit, I have a problem," that's when they move on to the next phase of the buyer's journey—the engagement phase. In the epiphany phase, buyers are seeking. In the engagement phase, buyers are searching.

Understand when you're in the engagement phase, you are not looking to buy anything. You've just switched from a passive to an active learning mode. You're now probably looking for things that build upon your confirmation bias for what was established in the first stage (which is again why that epiphany stage is so important in setting up the buyer's journey).

One of the common mistakes that sellers or marketers make is when they act as though, just because someone is engaged with something, it must mean they want to *buy* that something. Sales and marketing that jumps to a product-centric or sales-centric message too quickly won't effectively influence the engagement phase.

What's actually happening in the engagement phase is the potential customer is searching for information. They're looking to try to understand their issue better, and they're socializing around three elements: identifying the problem, exploring the solution, and defining what's needed. The searching and understanding part is the logical part. What's often missed (which you need to account for in your process mapping) is the socializing part.

Everybody's worried they're the only people that are thinking what they're thinking. They're not, but that's the isolation that comes from a lack of socializing during the engagement phase. Making it easy for people to share the ideas that you're a part of is a crucial component to moving toward the third stage.

What's happening in the engagement phase is the buyer is prioritizing. Where does this fit in the realm of everything else going on in my world? How does it help me? How does it hurt me?

The next question you want them to think about is, "Do I need to do something about it?"

If the answer to that question is "yes," you have reached the next stage of the buyer's journey.

THIRD STAGE: INTENT

The intent phase is typically the shortest phase. It's the point where a buyer is asking, "Do I need to do something about it?"

If you think of this phase from the perspective of a business, this is when you're determining if the juice is worth the squeeze. The third stage is when you're assessing whether the problem is big enough to warrant an investment in action, whether that be a complex sale or a large purchase.

A major missed opportunity that leads to decision reluctance is the doubt a buyer experiences when they wonder to themself, "Is this problem really such a big deal?" The mistake that businesses make is thinking that, because they understand the consequence of the problem, surely the customers also understand the consequence of the problem. This understanding should be clearly communicated, not left up to assumptions.

The first level of intent is the decision to investigate the problem. At this point, the operative question that needs to be answered is "Is the problem big enough?" The second level of intent is the commitment to do something about it. Both of these determinations fall within the intent phase of the buyer's journey, but they're very different perspectives.

Far too often, I've seen selling organizations spend all their time trying to demonstrate that they're the best choice. However, it's important to remember that being the best is not enough. You need to be the best and the *safest* choice for the potential buyer.

Being the best is about eliminating the problem. Being the safest is about eliminating the fear.

Addressing every level of the intent phase is how you position yourself as both the best and safest choice for buyers.

FOURTH STAGE: SELECTION PROCESS

After establishing intent, a potential customer enters the fourth phase, the selection process.

Here's the thing to understand about the selection process (otherwise known as the decision process): **You do not win business during the selection phase. You can only lose it.**

During the selection phase, the buyer is seeking validation, building consensus internally, and narrowing suppliers down. Now, this doesn't mean business can only be won if you're deeply involved in the pre-decision or pre-selection phases. It just means that once a potential customer has hit the selection phase, they've already set their longitude and latitude. They've set the path that they're on, and they're seeking validation far more than they're seeking new information. If you can align to what they're looking for, you can win.

To some degree, it's everybody's dream to build demand in this way. HubSpot did a great job of this, actually. They were the ones who created the need for inbound marketing. Then people started looking for inbound marketing. Of course, HubSpot looked like the safest choice; they were there for inbound marketing. That's what brought on scale.

When you take a closer look at this case, HubSpot was able to "suddenly" generate demand because of all the work they did in the epiphany, engagement, and intent phases, culminating in their win in the selection phase.

But the buyer's journey doesn't end here.

FIFTH STAGE: HAPPINESS

The happiness stage is very often what triggers the next iteration of the buyer's journey. This phase is all about judging. A buyer will inevitably return to their heuristics and judge whether a good decision was made or not.

I cannot count how many times I've seen selling organizations do a fantastic job all the way up to the selection phase…and then stop. They thought the buyer's journey was over once they were chosen over their competitors, and they were wrong.

Stopping at the selection stage creates a drag on growth efforts because reinforcing and reaffirming the decision increases the likelihood that people will share their experiences. This generates the greatest marketing of all time: buyer-to-buyer word of mouth. Even worse, when you stop right after the buyer decides on your product, the positive feelings a buyer gets from their decision will erode over time.

My brother, Donald Davidoff, actually wrote a book *Contact: Customer Service in the Hospitality and Tourism Industry.* The focus is on customer satisfaction, and he includes a formula for satisfaction.

Satisfaction = Perception – Expectation

If you don't set clear expectations that can be confirmed after the selection phase, then you cannot determine a clear sense of satisfaction or happiness in the fifth phase.

Metaphorically, we tend to think of the buyer's journey as a straightforward walk from problem to purchase. But it's really the snowball in a pinball machine. The larger the snowball, the more predictable the movement of the sale. The smaller the snowball, the less predictable.

It's important to note that, especially in business sales, there are multiple people involved in the buying process. This means that there are multiple journeys and each person involved can be at a different phase. The role of the seller (the salesperson and their organization) is to enable the alignment between the varying perspectives, experiences, and expectations.

This is why it is so advantageous to be present as early as possible in the journey; it allows the rapport between your business and your buyers to build. If I were a potential customer who only had one or two interactions with you because I started engaging with you at the end of my buyer's journey, you wouldn't have the same presence or command of the situation as if I'd been following your company blog for two and a half years and I'm primed to do something about a problem that you're positioned to solve for me.

I'm not saying you need to take two and a half years when you could do it in less time, but you should avoid the mentality of jumping in right before people buy. With a short-sighted process like that, you end up with a small snowball and a lot less influence over the buyer's decision than you would have otherwise had.

TIPS AND TAKEAWAYS

In Chapter 13, we covered the first component of approach: process. To create a strong process for your organization, you must:

- Avoid common pitfalls of weak processes, such as rigidity and vagueness,
- Be able to map your process from interest to revenue,
- And be present as early as possible in the buyer's journey in order to build a bigger snowball.

Approach is how you manifest the invisible structure and systems within your organization into a visible process. In other words, processes are important to the results of your approach, and contribute greatly to the ultimate goal of revenue acceleration: getting more juice for the squeeze.

CHAPTER 14

METHODOLOGY

OFTENTIMES, WHEN I TALK TO COMPANIES ABOUT THEIR APPROACH and I talk about processes and methodologies, I get blank stares. If there's someone in the room who's brave enough to ask, I'll get a question like, "What's the difference?"

A lot of people confuse process and methodology for the same thing, and while these two components are strongly related, there is a clear and important distinction to be made. A process represents the value chain; it's comprised of steps, stages, and/or milestones. Your process defines what you are doing. A methodology is how people move between those steps, stages, or milestones. In essence, process is what you do and methodology is how it's done.

The process is the map. The methodology is the style.

To further understand the difference between process and methodology, let's take a tangent and talk about music. What can Bach, Beethoven, Bruce Springsteen, and Eminem teach you about growth? The answer—a topic I wrote about in a similarly titled blog post in November of 2009—has to do with the constraints of music.

There are only 12 notes in music, and somewhere around 70 percent of all music is composed from just 5 of those 12 notes. This fact blows my mind every time I think about it. When you consider just how much music is being put out there every single day, it's crazy how much variance comes from the same 12 notes. Every composer and musician has only 12 notes to work with. Bach and Beethoven worked with the same 12 notes as any modern musician. Yet, no one would confuse Bach, Beethoven, Bruce Springsteen, Bob Dylan, or Eminem. They're all pulling from the same pool of 12 notes, and they're producing fundamentally different outcomes.

That's the difference between process and methodology: The 12 notes are the process. The music is the methodology.

Music theorists will tell you that it's the limited number of notes that reveals the genius of composition. We would probably have less great music if there were a thousand different notes; more options doesn't guarantee greater outcomes. It's the same with genius businesses. The businesses that do the best are the ones who understand the simple elements of the process and can work it with methodology to create masterpieces.

While I love technology, it has a downside to it. One of the primary downsides is that it makes it too easy to keep things too complicated. As the late Steve Jobs, cofounder of Apple, has said, "That's been one of my mantras—focus and simplicity. Simple can be harder than complex; you have to work hard to get your thinking clean and to make it simple." When it comes to growth, simple is important,

Methodology is the second component of approach. It is your style, and it's how you do what you do.

KNOWING YOUR MODELS

If you don't have the methodology, you never know if you're doing things right or wrong. The only thing you can really judge is the outcome. Without a methodology, you'll find yourself at the end of the process and, candidly, you won't know how the hell you got there.

The first thing you must do to understand your methodology is connect it to your go-to-market model. Yes, that does mean you should know what your go-to-market strategy is by the time you develop your approach. By this point, you should know your economic model, your sales model, and your sales structure.

I've worked with many companies that follow the same basic process, but you would never know the difference. The process that we put our clients through is the same every time. We've got maybe three variations of it, but it's fundamentally the same process. Yet, one of the most frequent comments we get is how customized the experience feels for our clients. That's because our service is designed to get the right plan for each client.

But the only way we're able to achieve that degree of customization is because we have a clear process and a clear methodology to our approach with each client. Every time I've been convinced to make an exception to our underlying process or methodology, it's never worked out well for us or the company we're working with.

The right methodology for your business's sales model or economic model is going to be very, very different for somebody else. So, you can't just copy another winning company; you've got to understand your game.

YOU CAN'T CHANGE INTENT

Intent is a powerful mechanism. Luckily, it's not a confusing mechanism to master, and there's actually a very simple formula to determine the purchase element and figure out if people will buy from you. That formula is:

Engagement + Intent = Purchase

If I'm a customer who is actively engaged with your messaging, and I've got a high level of intent, there is a strong likelihood that I'm going to buy from you. On the flipside, if I don't have intent, then it doesn't matter how great your product or service is. I'm not going to buy from you no matter what you do. I'd hate to say this to all the superstar salespeople and visionary CEOs out there, but this is the harsh truth. There's not much you can do to influence somebody's intent.

But, we must remember that people buy on their terms; people buy on their timeline. This is also one of the reasons that so much discounting drives me crazy, especially when we're looking at larger opportunities. Seriously, do you think a 30 percent discount is going to change a buyer's intent?

Intent is pretty structural and, again, you can't influence it that much. Intent is pretty fixed in any given market, and it's not very discretionary. As I said before, 90 to 95 percent of your market isn't looking to do anything one way or the other. At any given time, only 5 to 10 percent of your market has any intent.

So, one of the trends you might've already noticed is that when you first start doing something, when you first launch that new initiative, there's a positive burst. We see this in the startup community all the time. They come out of the gate fast and everything's going great at first. This is because they come out with an offer that's aligned with the intent of their potential customers. In today's modern demand generation and modern marketing world, digital marketing prays at the altar of intent. Social media marketing, Google search algorithms—any number of these underlying elements—are striving to identify purchasing intent.

Going back to the process of your approach, finding people with intent is great because you will generate quicker sales with people whose intent you align with. But you cannot drastically create or change that intent.

What we see oftentimes when companies are reliant on high-intent markets is discounting and significant margin pressure. Communicating to intent-based markets shows limited results because intent is structural. So, as you get bigger, you need to generate higher volumes of leads. Early on, you will likely be generating more leads from high-intent people than low-intent people because they're more likely to respond quickly. But as your lead volume increases, the percentage of that pool with high-intent buyers will decrease significantly.

And if you try to engage with someone who has low (or no) intent in the same way that you do with somebody with high intent...as my dad used to say, it's like trying to teach a pig how to sing. It won't work, and you'll only end up annoying the pig.

ACQUISITION PROCESSES

Not everything is unknown or unchangeable, though. There is an actionable science to growth, and that science is based on three underlying acquisition processes that your methodology should touch upon.

The first acquisition process is what I call **engagement acquisition**. That's getting people to be aware of you, to pay attention to you, and to engage with you and your ideas. I think we can all agree that if someone's not aware of you, they're not going to buy from you.

The second acquisition, **customer acquisition**, gets the majority of attention in the world of growth. Like the term implies, customer acquisition is about winning the customer. Customers are important because they're the underlying asset that enables you to generate revenue. If we think back on how this is explained in the economic model: when you acquire a customer, you're acquiring an asset with the potential to produce revenue. However, while my economic model might say that the average lifetime of a customer is seven years, those years are only the potential lifetime until that customer has actually been with me for seven years.

Customer acquisition is also frequently conflated with the third form of acquisition—**revenue acquisition**. Sometimes, when you acquire the customer, you acquire the revenue. But increasingly these days, you don't. Subscription businesses are a great example of the difference between customer and revenue acquisition. If I signed a contract with you today to pay a subscription fee, maybe I would only pay one month out of what could have been a full 12 months of fees. So, the revenue acquisition process is where you actually generate your revenue; revenue acquisition is about customer management and keeping the asset you acquired that produces revenue.

THE PRINCIPLE AND POWER OF LIFT

Have you ever been in a plane and stopped for a moment and thought, "How the hell does this thing get up here, and what the heck is keeping it up here?"

The reason the plane stays in the sky, despite all the violations of common sense that indicate a giant tube of metal wouldn't be airborne for very long, is because of a very basic principle of physics—lift.

If the velocity of the air above a wing is greater than the velocity of the air below the wing, then it will create a vacuum above the wing, generating lift. This is why wings are curved, so there's a longer path for air to travel above the wing than below it. That, in a nutshell, is the basic principle of lift.

Let's apply "lift" to growing a business. If you want to scale, if you want to be able to grow consistently, then you need to generate engagement at a higher rate than you're generating new customers. Remember, if I'm not engaged with you, I'm not buying from you. So, the maximum number of people that could buy from you is however many people are engaged with you.

And, we know we're only going to get a small percentage of those people anyway, right? Then as you acquire more of the right type of customers, customers whose intent your services or products align with, you will generate a broader base of revenue-producing opportunities.

Because of recency bias, we tend to over-focus on customer acquisition or revenue acquisition at the expense of engagement, and this conflicts with the power of lift. As you're laying out the steps of your processes and defining your methodologies, you need to be paying attention to all three acquisition phases.

How are you generating engagement that turns into intent? How are you turning intent into customers, and how are you turning customers into revenue? I'd like to be able to tell anyone reading this book what their exact methodology should look like. But I'm not a magician.

I am, however, familiar with how frameworks can help you develop the methodology unique to your business.

DEVELOPING YOUR METHODOLOGY

There are five phases inherent in the process of engagement, customer, and revenue acquisition that you should remember when developing your methodology. At Imagine, we call this The D.E.A.L.S. Framework™:

Discover. There are a multitude of methodologies out there that you can use exclusively or interchangeably to find your customers and ensure that your customers can find you.

Engage. Understand how your methodology develops engagement between people and your organization. How do you distribute your content and your ideas? How do you create what I call the "first action?"

Activate. Five years ago, I realized why I needed to write this book; there was something wrong with the direction of the game so many companies were playing. Databases were getting bigger than they'd ever been before. Lead generation was performing at rates that previously we could only dream of. But nothing was fundamentally changing. When we generate leads, we're only generating the first point of engagement. What we fail to do is activate. As part of the buying and learning process, our methodology should enable us to socialize and engage with and activate our leads.

Launch. How do we generate customers? How does our sales process work? Use your methodology to support your process and understand your customers' buying experience.

Success. Finally, your methodology should enable the customer to be the hero of their own story. How does your product or service enable that success for your customers?

You get to define all these elements when you develop your methodology. Combining it with a clear sales process makes an effective approach even easier to manifest.

TIPS AND TAKEAWAYS

In Chapter 14, we covered the second component of approach: methodology. To develop your business's methodology, you must:

- First, differentiate between process (the map) and methodology (the style),
- Accept that buyer's intent remains unchangeable in most markets because people buy on their own terms,
- And follow an effective framework for your methodology, such as Imagine's D.E.A.L.S. framework.

Your methodology is your modus operandi. It's the unique component of your approach that you must develop for yourself. The methodology embodies the mystical element within every successful, winning company that people align themselves with.

CHAPTER 15

PLAYBOOKS

IN A PREVIOUS CHAPTER, I TOLD THE STORY ABOUT THE NEW England Patriots winning the Super Bowl over the Atlanta Falcons. Now, imagine that during the huddle for that game, the cameraman zoomed in on the Patriots and you see Tom Brady with his palm out.

He looks at Julian Edelman and he takes his right index finger to draw a line on his left palm. With a very serious expression, he says, "Okay, Julian, you run down here. See that lady in the yellow dress? You cut left there. No, not that yellow dress. The other one. Yup." Brady raises his palm higher so the whole team can see him drawing more invisible lines on his hand. "And Danny, you go down here until you get to the guy wearing the bright blue cap. When you get to that guy, cut right."

For many of us, this would be an odd mental image to process. (Although, when I was a kid, this is exactly how I'd play football in the street with my friends.)

Granted, if Tom Brady was running his NFL team by drawing the plays out in the palm of his hand during a game, he'd still be a pretty good quarterback. Probably. But he wouldn't be Tom Brady. And I bet whoever lets a team run with that approach wouldn't last very long in the NFL either. It's foolish to even think about, because the moment the ball gets put into play, a series of otherwise unexpected things will happen, and everybody has to adjust in orchestration with what their teammates are doing. It's an amazing feat to watch, and not something that can be planned out on the palm of the hand.

So, what makes that level of orchestration possible? The playbook. The playbook brings to light the many factors that need to harmonize with each other to enable success within a game, within an organization. Every person has a playbook; we all have a way that we do things. The problem is, more often than not, it's in our head.

Is the playbook you're operating from the same as everybody else's playbook within your organization? For the companies that want to see sustainable future growth, the answer to that question must uncontrovertibly be "yes."

THE FIVE FAILURES AND THREE ARCHETYPES OF PLAYBOOKS

Despite the crucial role of playbooks in both approach and organizational alignment, they have a bad rep in the business world, and I can understand why.

Early in my sales career, I remember everyone talking about playbooks. But then, for the next 20 or 25 years, they just totally disappeared. And the reason wasn't because playbooks weren't necessary when establishing one's approach; it was because, quite frankly, those early playbooks kind of sucked.

Even today, most playbooks that get implemented will fail. But that doesn't mean the playbooks themselves are bad. Much like the failure of processes, the failure of playbooks is caused by the poor implementation of the thing rather than the thing itself, and I've identified five main causes for this failure.

The first problem is they're not built for use. I remember, during the first sales job I had, I was given a playbook. Now this was back in the old days when everything had to be printed. The first playbook that I was handed had this beautiful white spiral binding and a nice-looking cover with one of those transparencies on the front. There were about 35 pages in this company's playbook, printed neatly in 11 point font, and you know where I put it? The second drawer of my desk, the same place everyone else at the company put it. I don't know what the status of my old desk is, but I wouldn't be surprised if that playbook's still in its second drawer. No one has ever taken that playbook out of the drawer and used it to figure out what's going on in the company now.

Sure, the formatting has been updated in recent years. Playbooks have modernized. Now they're distributed as PDFs. But if you're expecting that people will open the document to learn anything, I can tell you now it won't happen. The reason that you create the playbook is so that the playbook gets built into the organization's systems. If they're not built for reference, they won't get referenced.

Reason number two, the playbooks are either too rigid or vague. This is the same issue as why processes fail. A lack of clear but flexible parameters to define the playbook will leave you with a bad playbook.

The third reason that they fail is that they're internally focused. At best, those failed playbooks focus on how we sell, when they really should be focused on how we interact with how buyers buy. Your goal should not be to make a sale. Your goal should be enabling potential customers to make good decisions. Remember, we're managing a decision process far, far more than we're managing a sales process.

Number four, many playbooks are built with false assumptions. They're built based on how we want things to work, not on how they work. They're built on artificial ideas, like the idea you should make the sale in two meetings. When in reality, it could take 23 meetings to make the sale. (As a side note, I'm not saying every sale takes 23 meetings. I'm just saying sometimes that's what it takes, right?)

If you want a playbook that works, it needs to reflect reality.

The final main reason why playbooks fail is because they're not built for iteration. A playbook should never be "done." It needs to be a living, breathing tool. In other words, adaptation is the key to progress.

The sign of a good team is one where the players know to make adjustments during the season. If I'm coaching a football team, I want to see my team do better in the second half of the season than they do in the first half of the season. And if you happen to be a sports fan, you and I both know it's a hell of a lot better if your favorite team is hot at the end of the season, rather than the start of the season.

If you can avoid those five common failures, you're one step closer to building an effective playbook that maximizes the opportunity for you to win your game. When it comes to effective playbooks, there are three archetypes you could choose from, depending on the game you're trying to win.

The first one's what I call programmatic, which is typically a playbook designed for high-speed short cycles. It's best for high volume, short sales cycles, short decision cycles, and typically lower prices or lower margins. This is your mass market playbook.

The second kind of playbook is what I refer to as the "target and cultivate" playbook. This is an archetype designed for a sale that involves more complexity with moderate-to-long sales cycles or decision cycles. This is best for longer and higher consideration periods.

And the third type of playbook is the account-focused or "named accounts" playbook, which is for very large opportunities that require long and very complex decision cycles.

CONTINUOUS VS. DISCONTINUOUS INNOVATION

From a company perspective, these three types of playbooks are not mutually exclusive. And, as a matter of fact, a lot of companies need to run multiple playbooks at a time. There's nothing wrong with having multiple playbooks. What's actually bad for business is trying to run one playbook for everything.

Different games require different playbooks, and one of the factors that can help you determine which playbooks to use is understanding the form of innovation your business offers to customers.

Continuous innovation is innovation where the benefit that the customer picks up comes without the customer really having to do anything. They don't have to change, learn, think differently or do differently. Imagine for a moment if I invented a new refrigerator that had twice the storage capacity and used half the energy and fit in the exact same footprint as your existing refrigerator. That's a pretty easy decision for you to make. You either need a refrigerator with more storage space or you don't. And if you do choose to buy, you don't need to relearn how to use the refrigerator.

Discontinuous innovation is when the customer has to change to be able to take full advantage of the offered benefits. If I were trying to sell you on a new piece of software, you could potentially gain a lot out of the purchase, but only if you learned how to adopt and use the software appropriately.

Continuous innovation moves us toward simpler and programmatic playbooks. Discontinuous innovation moves us toward "target and cultivate" or "named accounts" playbooks. And that's not the only factor to consider when picking the right playbook(s).

PICKING YOUR PLAYBOOKS

What's your average sale value? A smaller sale favors a more programmatic playbook. A larger sale value requires something more custom.

What type of offer are you selling? Are you selling a product or a service? While a product could apply to all three playbooks, it's easier to be programmatic with a product than a service.

Is it a simple sale or a complex sale? Are one or two people involved in the decision, or are multiple people and factors involved? The former would tend toward programmatic playbooks, while the complex sale may require a custom playbook.

What's your positioning? Are you a leader in the market, or a challenger? Programmatic playbooks are largely ineffective if people don't already know who you are.

Where are you in the product life cycle? Are you selling to the early side, the majority, or the late majority market? Programmatic playbooks are more in tune with the majority and late majority markets, while "target and cultivate" and "named accounts" playbooks suit the earlier side of the product life cycle.

Where are you trying to connect with people on the purchase cycle (buyer's journey)? Programmatic playbooks only work with post-intent markets. So if you're going to do programmatic, is there enough intent in the market to support what you're doing?

What is the length of your customers' purchase cycle? Are your products or services something that must be revisited regularly, or is it something that buyers sign five-year contracts for? The more frequently someone purchases, the more likely programmatic will fit the sale. The less frequent the sales, or the more infrequent the purchase cycles, the more likely you will need to adopt a more custom playbook.

The tables below illustrate which archetypes are best suited to address which factors of the sales process. Once you familiarize yourself with these factors, you will be equipped to build the most effective playbooks for your business's sales approach.

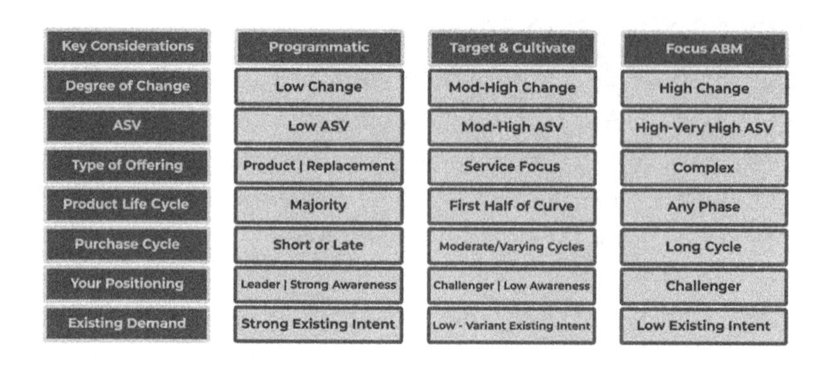

Key Considerations	Programmatic	Target & Cultivate	Focus ABM
Degree of Change	Low Change	Mod-High Change	High Change
ASV	Low ASV	Mod-High ASV	High-Very High ASV
Type of Offering	Product | Replacement	Service Focus	Complex
Product Life Cycle	Majority	First Half of Curve	Any Phase
Purchase Cycle	Short or Late	Moderate/Varying Cycles	Long Cycle
Your Positioning	Leader | Strong Awareness	Challenger | Low Awareness	Challenger
Existing Demand	Strong Existing Intent	Low - Variant Existing Intent	Low Existing Intent

TIPS AND TAKEAWAYS

In Chapter 15, we covered the third component of approach: playbooks. To choose the best playbooks for your business, you must:

- Create playbooks that reflect reality and are made to be used, not stored in a desk,
- Understand the form of innovation (continuous versus discontinuous) that your business offers its customers,
- And pick the appropriate playbooks depending on the complexity of the game you're playing.

A good approach can only happen when the people within your organization are working off of the same playbooks. In fact, through a strong cohesion of process, methodology, and playbooks, you can create an approach that will enable a greater execution of your growth and RevOps objectives with less effort.

PART V

PUTTING IT INTO ACTION

CHAPTER 16

EXECUTION AND PERFORMANCE

I'VE BEEN A FAN OF BUSINESS SINCE I WAS A KID. I GREW UP AS the son of entrepreneurs. My parents owned a travel agency, and my dad was the president of the American Society of Travel Agents (ASTA). From a young age, I knew that in one way, shape, or form, I was going to own my own business one day.

As an adult, I've always followed the business press with the same interest as I used to follow the sports section, and I've read many books and stories about the history of companies. But the one story I've never read is one where a CEO gives a rousing speech to a group of analysts about how the new strategy they are implementing, if carried out successfully, will end within the next three to five years in bankruptcy.

Despite never seeing a company plan to execute a bankruptcy, we see companies go bankrupt every day.

In the beginning of my early career in sales, I used to think companies that went bankrupt weren't any good at business. They must not have any product or service worth buying. They must not have any ideas worth investing in. But later on, I learned that the primary reason for a business's failure was a bit more nuanced than, "Oh, they must suck at this."

If you look at the difference between companies that have had blowout success and companies that *were* successful but then struggled or never got off the ground, the difference is not in the brilliance of the ideas or the competency of the people or products. The difference often came down to execution.

THE LUCKY DIFFERENCE

Back in April 2018, I had the opportunity to interview Steve Pao on my podcast, *The Black Line between Sales and Marketing*.

Steve is a super interesting guy. He's a chemical engineer by background, and he's also run marketing for several companies from startup through IPO success. He was the first head of product management for Barracuda Networks, which is one of the most successful internet infrastructure companies in history. They were one of the first companies that took on addressing email spam, and their big product back in the day was email firewalls. Steve also headed marketing for Latitude Communications, which was eventually bought by Cisco. And, at the time of our interview, he was running marketing for a highly funded startup by the name of Igneous.

So, Steve had an interesting experience because not only was he involved in Barracuda (which by all definitions was a runaway success of a company), he was also involved in a heavily funded startup that failed so miserably that they ended up returning a good portion of their money back to their investors.

Steve was the perfect person I could ask the question, "What's the difference between a company that has blowout success and a company that fails so miserably it doesn't even get a chance to spend all the money that was invested?"

And I'll never forget Steve's answer. He simply said, "Luck."

It was an answer that only a chemical engineer-type person would give. Certainly, nobody with an MBA would provide this answer, but it's actually the truth. Steve went on to mention that the people who worked at the startup that didn't succeed were every bit as smart and capable as the people who worked at Barracuda, and the product of the failed startup was every bit as strong as its competitors.

He brought up a really interesting point about Barracuda's success. The product that really made the company what it is today was that initial email firewall. And Barracuda had been there just as email was becoming the communication du jour. He said candidly that if the product had launched three to six months earlier, or three to six months later, no one would have ever heard of Barracuda. Their product hit at the right time. And that's the truth for most businesses, right?

The word pivot has become trite. That's how frequently the strategy that an organization implements fails to deliver on its expectations.

THE THREE GO-TO-MARKET GAME TYPES

One of the most important lessons that I've shared in this book is that success is more about how you're doing what you're doing and how you adjust than it is about the initial setting or strategy.

In other words, you need to be maniacally focused on defining, adapting to, and executing within your game. When I first got into advising companies on growth initiatives, I referred to the first step of the process that I followed as the "define your game" step. How you define your game is one of the most important decisions that you'll ever make.

From a broad perspective, there are three games (you may call them strategies or approaches) that you can apply to winning and keeping high-value customers. These approaches exist as points along what I call the personalization continuum. The right game for you is dependent upon what you're selling, how you're selling, who your customers are, what they're buying, how they're buying, and basically everything that we talked about in the earlier chapters covering go-to-market strategy—your economic model, your sales model, etc.

The first game type is what I call the **programmatic** game type. This game is a one to two on the personalization continuum. It's the simplest and most common approach. The programmatic game utilizes very little personalization in terms of the messaging, tactics, and underlying processes being executed. It works best for smaller average sales values, if for no other reason than the economics of what you're selling. It works well when the product category or the service category that you're selling has well-defined and strong existing demand in the market. The programmatic game looks very similar to broad-based business-to-consumer companies, so it tends to be focused more on the product or service being offered than on unique needs. Programmatic games are also highly focused on leads, so they're very lead-centric. It highlights the features and benefits of what's being sold. It has the most traditional characteristics of what we think of when we think of sales and marketing.

The next game is what I call the **contextualized** game. This game is a three to five on the personalization continuum, and it's where account-focused approaches begin to separate themselves from lead-centric approaches. With a more contextualized, account-focused approach, you're modifying your tactics, message, and process based on meta elements like trends in the industry. While it is a step above programmatic games in terms of personalization, a contextualized game is still more industry-segmented than it is account-segmented. That's why it's kind of the middle game type. You're not individualizing your tactics and your messaging, but you are developing more specific flavors and themes based on different scenarios. Typically, a contextualized game will operate with three to seven kinds of messaging or tactical archetypes.

The contextualized game is best played when the one-size-fits-all model isn't sufficient to break through the noise, to generate the type of engagement or activation that's needed to influence your target accounts, or to demonstrate the impact of what you're doing to get your potential customers across the finish line. It works best in moderate to large average sales value models. It also works well when you're not a dominant leading player in your market, and the familiarity with your company or your offering isn't clear. It's the game that you need to play when there are multiple personas or multiple people involved in influencing a decision. The bottom line is, if you're involved in complex sales, you're going to need to play at least the contextualized game to have an adequate amount of personalization.

Since the contextualized game is more complicated than the programmatic game, it requires more effort. The payoff comes from greater predictability and higher margins. In contrast, the programmatic game works best if you have a low cost or commodity or you're positioning around a more commodity-type offering. If you are trying to position it as a premium or differentiated offering, you'll want to play the contextualized or the next game, the individualized.

The third game is **individualized**. This is the most complicated and difficult game to play, rating about a six to seven on the personalization continuum. It takes the contextualized game to the extreme. With this approach, you create custom tactics, custom messaging, even custom processes to break into, manage, and win specific accounts. This means messaging is at least account-specific, if not role-specific within the account. The individualized game is best played when you're selling to large companies and your product or service has a large average sales value. For example, if you want to sell a high-end product or service to Procter & Gamble, Walmart, and the like, a contextualized message about what is generally happening in the industry is not going to be enough. You need to design a message specifically geared toward your customer. Playing and winning the individualized game requires deep knowledge about your customer's world, what's unique about their environment, their challenges, and their opportunities.

If you know you will eventually need to play the individualized game but don't have enough knowledge to play the game well, you can start with the contextualized game and build from there. This brings us to an important question.

HOW MANY GAMES CAN YOU PLAY?

Despite the differences in execution, these games are not mutually exclusive. You don't have to choose just one. In fact, some companies run all three. In my experience, most companies should be playing two of the games, though that doesn't mean that you shouldn't be playing only one. What's really important isn't how many games you play; it's how you segment your market so that you're only playing one game with them.

What you need to do is determine what game you're playing with which customers in your addressable market. It's better to play fewer games well, than more games moderately. And that means that your marketing tactics and sales tactics should be designed, supported, managed, and measured within the context of the game that you're playing. The key to effective tactics is aligning behind a clear game.

Too often, I see companies going to market and trying to play one game across all their customers. In essence, they find the lowest common denominator and play to that.

As an example of a classic mistake in game selection:

Several years ago, when inbound marketing was emerging, research done by HubSpot showed that blogging had a tremendous impact on the ability of a company to position itself strongly. Further, the data showed that the more often a company blogged, the more leads the company developed and the lower the cost per.

So what did companies do? They started blogging.

I remember getting calls from companies who were saying, "We're looking to blog three to five times per week."

And when we asked, "What do you want to write about?"

They'd hit us with, "Well, we're looking for you to help us figure that out." And whenever I got a response like this, I knew that company was a prospect that I wanted to stay away from.

Seeing that something worked for somebody else is not the reason for you to do it.

If you take a look at the data that seemed to prove the correlation between increased blogging and increased leads, that research was done *before* the correlation was identified. So what you found was the people who blogged more frequently in the early days of blogging actually had relevant things to say. The mistake that gets made is when we turn a 300-word blog post into a 3,000-word post. What happens if no new or relevant content gets added to the lengthened blog?

To have confidence in a tactic or game, you want to ask a very simple question: Does it create value for the customer? Realize that value is a measurement of someone being willing to pay for something.

Do you want to know if your marketing is effective? Ask yourself, "Would the people in my target market be willing to pay to look at my market?"

Want to assess whether your salespeople are conducting effective discoveries and sales calls? Ask yourself, "Would the prospect have been willing to pay for the sales call after the salesperson made it?"

Now, I'm not suggesting that you start charging for your marketing or your sales calls. (Although...I'm not suggesting that you *don't* do that either.) What I'm saying is your customers are paying one way or the other with the most expensive resource they have, and that resource is their attention.

STEPPING OUT OF YOUR SYSTEM

We're all self-centered. We like to think that we're not, but the truth is that we are. The great news is that being self-centered isn't necessarily bad. The danger with being self-centered in business and when going to market is that we often think that we're thinking about the customer when we're really not. To be able to execute effectively, you have to be able to step outside of yourself, your organization, and your system.

In the late 1800s, philosopher and mathematician Kurt Gödel created his first incompleteness theorem, which said:

You cannot judge a system from within that system.

Likewise, you can't judge your tactics, your processes, or your playbook from within that system. You must be able to break away and look at what you're doing from the outside.

How are we solving for the customer? Even if they never buy from us, talk to us, or consider working with us in the future? Your customers, and potential customers, have all the control. While many people will tell you that's a new concept, it's really not. Customers have always had all the control. Today, they just have far more choices for how they want to handle things. Your job then is to figure out how to solve their problems in every aspect of your go-to-market.

Building revenue today is hard. It's really, really hard. The last 15 to 20 years have wiped out the fish—the chumps at the poker table that everybody made easy money off of. The bad competition out there doesn't really exist anymore. Furthermore, technology has changed the underlying parameters of how businesses compete, eliminating the cost advantages that small and mid-market companies had on their larger competitors in the past. For mid-market companies in the current business environment, building revenue means you've got to go against gravity.

That gravitational pull is trying to reduce the perceived value and impact that your company brings. To win, you must present a distinct position in the market.

THE 80/20 RULE

In business, you might've heard of the 80/20 rule, something about how 80 percent of your business comes from 20 percent of your customers. I've always hated that rule.

If 80 percent of your business or profit is coming from 20 percent of your customers, what about the other 80 percent of your customers? Why are you selling to them? Why not generate more business from your 20 percent? Why not find more companies that look and feel and act like your 20 percent?

If you look at the game that I play, I would rather lose a piece of business that I could win than win a piece of business that I shouldn't. Because if I win a piece of business that I shouldn't, that's going to drag all the other results. Imagine is playing a game with a high level of personalization, so we're higher-priced. We're not managing low-end products.

If you are just okay, if distinction doesn't matter, the Amazons of the world are going to eat your lunch. You might be able to make a living, but you're not going to generate wealth. Amazon doesn't win by being the best option for everybody. It's just never the worst option. The businesses that win tomorrow will either be the ones that represent the best choice or the ones that represent the lowest price.

This is what I mean by stepping out of your system:

Throw out the playbook that gives you an outcome where 80 percent of your customers are giving you 20 percent of your business.

That's a terrible way to do business, even though it's a natural thing to do, and everybody does it. But you don't have to. Step outside of your system and think about how you get to a place where every one of your customers is the best customer.

EXECUTION IS MESSY

If you are aiming to win—if you're aiming to achieve the type of success and the type of growth that you're likely looking for by reading this book—it's going to come down to your ability to execute. Execution is tough, and that's for a few reasons.

First of all, execution is messy. The thing that's "neat" about developing strategy and vision is that you get to work in a metaphorical laboratory. Everything is clean. Everything is clear. Everything is controlled. However, execution is about the world outside the laboratory. Things are constantly changing in reality; therefore the rhythms, the harmonies, the synchronicity, the orchestration for strategy and for execution are very, very different.

In my experience, when people talk about the pursuit of alignment, what they're really talking about is synchronizing the rhythms of strategy with the rhythms of execution. The intent is to create strong feedback systems so as you're executing, it's feeding into and adjusting your strategy. And as you're strategizing, it's feeding into and adjusting your execution. This helps to maintain a balance between getting the work done that needs to be done and iterating to sustain growth and improvements.

To be clear, this book is not about tactics; this is a book about frameworks. I have specifically worked to avoid diving too deeply into any specific topic. For those of you who might want to know how to implement tactics within your business's framework, there are tons of great resources out there that enable deeper dives, many of which I've listed in a resource section at the end of this book.

For now, here's the thing you need to understand about tactics. You could show me any tactic and I'll be able to give you a list of companies that have executed the tactic well and succeeded. I'll also be able to give you a list of companies that have executed the tactic effectively and failed. The key factor that's going to determine your outcomes isn't what specific tactics you pick. It's going to be how you are willing to implement, and change, those tactics in the context of your market situation.

THE ROLE OF DISRUPTION AND WAYNE GRETZKY

Much earlier in this book, I referenced Jack Welch's famous quote, "If the rate of change on the outside exceeds the rate of change on the inside, the end is near."

...and holy cow is the rate of change outside our organizations getting faster.

We live in a disruptive environment, but disruption isn't new; all of this disrupting and shifting isn't unique to the 21st century. When the agricultural age gave way to the Industrial Age, the agricultural system fought hard to protect itself, because that's what the status quo does. It fights to protect itself and stay the same. If it didn't do that, it wouldn't be much of a status quo.

However, the Industrial Age got a huge boost with World War II. Think about it. Every leading country, with the exception of the United States, had been mostly destroyed, and their manufacturing bases were eliminated. The Marshall Plan was created to rebuild the Western world with America as its base and, as hard as the status quo of the agricultural system held on, the Industrial Revolution persisted with specialized production and other new concepts that allowed corporate entities to form and grow on a mass scale. It was around this time that America became a true economic force coming into modern times.

Then, the Industrial Age gave way to the Information Age, and the status quo fought hard to protect itself again. It's a cycle that we see repeating itself to this day. Today and into the future, we're experiencing a paradigm shift where yesterday's game is fighting to stay relevant. Even before we got to this internet age, we saw supply growing at a faster and faster rate. We've moved from a supply-constrained market to a demand-constrained market. We moved from a *caveat emptor* (buyer beware) where the seller controlled the game, to today where it's *caveat venditor* (seller beware) and the buyer controls the game.

Your buyers have more choices in the products, services, and other offerings than they could ever use. Consequently, you need to push beyond the status quo and adapt competitively to be able to play your game and win. You need to transform your approach.

And here's the interesting thing about disruption. Disruption is not about today, and it's certainly not about yesterday. Disruption is all about tomorrow.

To win in disruptive environments, you need to be obsessed with where you're going. Think like the greatest hockey player in the history of the world, Wayne Gretzky. "Skate to where the puck is going. Not where it has been." While Gretzky wasn't the biggest or strongest guy on the ice, he understood the game and played it better than anyone else in history.

Now, I'm not saying you have to be the business equivalent of Wayne Gretzky in order to win. What I am saying is that, in business, you need to share Gretzky's philosophy to sustain growth in a disruptive world.

Focus on where you're going, and align yourself toward a future point.

BATTLING THE WHIRLWIND

There's actually a specific word for the type of change, the type of disruption, that I'm talking about. That word is transformation.

And one of the biggest challenges of transformation that mid-market and small companies face whenever they're implementing any improvement, effort, or change initiative is something I like to call the whirlwind.

Transformation represents change, and change is hard. The whirlwind is why transformations fail because the whirlwind is our day job. We've all got a job to do outside of the added work of changing what that job entails. Most people and organizations I've worked with are not struggling with an overabundance of time, right? Most people are already overwhelmed with what they have to do on a daily basis.

So when things like change initiatives and transformations and new technologies come in, it becomes one more thing that has to be done. And while visions can be great, visions are not strong enough to overcome the whirlwind. We've all got things to do. We've all got our routines and our ways of doing things. I've learned that one of the big advantages that large companies have (especially those global mega-billion organizations) is that they have groups and departments specifically set aside to do nothing but work on initiatives and improvement areas. The difficulty that small mid-market companies face is that we don't have that luxury of specialization.

The whirlwind represents what needs to be done now. It's the status quo. It's the power of inertia. It takes a surprising amount of energy and effort to get something started. So, part of the problem for both executives and individual contributors is that only two time periods naturally exist in the mind of the individual. Now and later. But in reality, later almost always means never. Whatever gets assigned for later stays in that indefinite future space forever.

In simpler terms, inertia is a bitch.

And so we make a critical mistake after we identify the systems we want to change and the problems we want to solve. We jump in and try to fix it without a sense of prioritization or focus.

Now, it took me a long time to learn this lesson because for years I had believed what many people believe, which is that the great advantage of being a small company is how agile and nimble they are. There are many times when being quick-moving is a great advantage. But when you're talking about creating the type of structure that enables you to sustain growth, there's a fine line between strength and weakness.

The challenge that smaller to mid-market companies face is that they, inadvertently and without realizing it, thrust too much change upon their people and systems. Or they try to do too much too fast. And the net result of all that uncontrolled and mismanaged disruption is that it overwhelms people and systems. All one needs to look at is engagement levels and exhaustion levels of the people working in business today to realize how overwhelmed they already are, before any change initiatives are even thrown at them.

A key mindset to have for RevOps is that you should not solve upstream problems downstream. You can also think of it as the tyranny of urgency. The "problem" with change and transformation is that, when done properly, it focuses on the important. But what is important will never win out over what is urgent unless there's a construct and framework in place to enable that prioritization to happen.

When we try to change too much, too fast, we get overwhelmed by the conflicting whirlwind of daily responsibilities. It multiplies complexity, and it's the opposite of velocity. We do more. We run faster. We make less progress.

Which is why we're going to discuss a model that can help you regain prioritization and focus in your execution.

THE THREE ZONES OF EXECUTION

The three zones of execution enable you to view change initiatives not only through the lens of importance, but also through the lens of time. This model enables you to build a clearer implementation path so that you're consistently making changes so you stay ahead of the curve, but not changing so much that you're getting overwhelmed and bogged down.

The three zones of execution are the performance zone, the enablement zone, and the transformation zone.

Going in reverse order, the third zone is the transformation zone, which is the period beyond a year. Transformation is a long-term endeavor and it doesn't happen overnight or in one or two steps, so the transformation zone is where your vision lives. It's where the big change initiatives are identified and the capabilities your company needs are built to win in the future. These are all anchored in the transformation zone. A strong transformation zone gives everybody a clear sense of purpose and direction. Some people call it the north star—a clear point that the people and systems of the organization can focus on. It enables the alignment that companies work so hard to achieve.

The second zone, the enablement zone, represents the period 90 days out to one year. It's what enables the vision to become a reality and buffers the sharp, jagged edges of change. This is where we stage our improvements. We systemize, standardize, and optimize. When the enablement zone is working well, you're able to bring significant change to the organization at rapid rates without ever thrusting too much change on the people within your company or the systems that are enabling them to perform.

The performance zone is all about now. It's the next 90 days. It's about meeting our short-term objectives and hitting the proverbial number. All results are achieved in the performance zone, but without a strong transformation zone and enablement zone, the performance zone won't have the capacity or ability to drive strong results on a continuous basis.

THE MISSING PIECE

After working with and analyzing easily more than a thousand small mid-market companies, I've determined that 95 percent have at least one thing in common, and that's the piece they're missing in their execution. That piece is the enablement zone.

Good companies typically have good to great visions. And if you're reading this book about revenue *growth*, you're probably executing pretty well already. In fact, most good companies have a strong vision, and they execute well, at least in good times. The problem is when they hit an inflection point. After growing, growing, and growing, they hit the point where what got them there isn't enough to get them any further. Sometimes, it can be a result of a shift in the market, or a shift in the economy. Regardless, they're unable to adjust effectively. They get stuck.

This is the critical reason why zones are important, because without effective prioritization of tasks, companies may not even realize the missing piece between what they're achieving today and what they hope to achieve in the future. The enablement zone is where the strength and resilience of go-to-market is built. This is where companies that have very good outcomes will often fail because they've got no real resilience. Most companies have a zone one and a zone three; they've got vision and they've got execution. What they don't have is that translation ground, that enablement zone.

Zone two is where consistency, sustainability, and predictability are created. Obviously, if you want to dynamically grow your business, you need consistency and sustainability. The enablement zone is the playground of revenue operations.

I'VE GOT 99 PROBLEMS, BUT PRIORITIZATION AND FOCUS AIN'T ONE

	Typical Time Frame	Focus of Activity
The Transformation Zone	1 – 3 Years	• Vision • Change Initiatives • Build Capabilities
The Enablement Zone	90 Days – 1 Year	• Stage • Operationalize • Systemize • Optimize
The Performance Zone	Next 90 Days	• Meet Objectives • Hit the Number

The three-zones approach enables you to map our organization's improvements in a way that is sustainable. To implement this approach, all you need to do is identify the action or initiative that needs to be taken and assign it to the appropriate zone, like I've done with the 17 example initiatives above. A visual marker of your three zones of execution can be an invaluable roadmap to success.

With effort on the X axis and time to impact on the Y axis, you create four quadrants that correlate with the three zones:

- Bottom left is zone one, for tasks that require low time and effort.
- Upper left and bottom right are zone two, for tasks that require either high time or high effort.
- Upper right is zone three, for tasks that require BOTH high time and effort.

I want to make it absolutely clear here that there is no "ideal" zone. Everything that is assigned to a zone should already be a task that would have gone on a linear to-do list for your business. The trick is establishing a clear path of execution that enables both prioritization and focus, which can be a challenge when things are put in a linear list. Luckily, that's not a challenge that you even need to face.

Most people tend to treat corporate planning like a linear list or outline, which would seem overwhelming from an organizational standpoint. A list provides no construct of time. There's no construct of weight. And I've seen this problem where, for example, the regular "pipeline cleanup" task and "expand to new verticals" initiative are put on the same list. That kind of conflation between frequent-task urgency and infrequent-task importance fries people's minds. As things get more robust, we need less of a list and more of an active roadmap.

The purpose of differentiating execution into zones is to ensure that the business can effectively prioritize its initiatives. While on a technical level, people can understand that different tasks are of varying importance, sometimes (actually, oftentimes) the task at the top of the list is not the most important; it's simply the most urgent. By creating zones of execution, rather than a list of tasks to execute, you're better able to allocate teams, systems, and resources to the right tasks *at the right time.*

For example, if you're a mid-market company, you have certain functions that are primarily zone one, such as your sales teams. Your senior team is typically zone three. Whatever is your long-term strategic planning would also be a zone three discipline. What you can begin to do once you've established your zone one and three functions is carve out different groups or percentages of time for people to move to zone two, the enablement zone, to bridge between the urgent tasks of today and the important tasks of tomorrow.

The grid provides a visual element that enables me to begin to filter and identify and know what's going on across the three zones, while the zones of execution help to further differentiate between important versus urgent initiatives. It includes important factors of prioritization for a business, like time and effort. When we implement initiatives according to a roadmap rather than a list, we avoid the problem of seeing everything as a top priority, which causes nothing to be a real priority.

ACCELERATION CYCLES

Be sure to give your efforts enough time to work, and be sure you don't wait too long to make an adjustment.

That's one of the smartest yet most frustrating pieces of advice I ever got early in my career. It's a great philosophy that encompasses the importance of deliberate, actionable change. But I didn't know initially how much time was "enough time." That's what led me to create the concept of acceleration cycles.

An acceleration cycle is very similar to an annual plan, and I should specify I mean an annual plan done *the right way*. (Because, frankly, most annual plans are a waste of time.)

When you come out of strategizing and planning in your laboratory, you've got a list (or, ideally, a roadmap) of things to do. This is the beginning of your acceleration cycle and execution of initiatives. If you have a 90-day acceleration cycle, you're determining what your objectives will be over the next 90 days, as well as your key metrics and the things you're looking to achieve, drive, and move.

Think of acceleration cycles the way a sailor would view a journey. If I'm a sailor and I'm going to start my journey in Annapolis and I'm trying to end it in Barcelona, Spain, I won't sail straight from Annapolis to Barcelona. I'll plot out waypoints along the journey. Each of those waypoints is like an acceleration cycle. As we reach each new waypoint, we reassess. Is the destination still the same? Are we on course? Have the conditions changed?

In an environment where things are constantly changing, it's hard to get invested in something if, every day, people come into work fearing an unexpected change. This is why I recommend an acceleration cycle to enable the right amount of opportunity for quick adjustment. Pairing an acceleration cycle with the three zones of execution creates more predictability and stability about when things get reassessed and changed within an organization.

For a vast majority of companies, I recommend an acceleration cycle of 90 days. If your business is in a hyper-growth mode, you may want to shorten your acceleration cycle to 30 days. We believe in most cases, 90 days is long enough to execute initiatives effectively, but not so long that you're digging yourself into a huge sinkhole of missed opportunities for adjustment. 90 days gives you flexibility and agility, but it also creates a clear path of execution.

I also recommend there be at least one adjustment period per acceleration cycle. In a 90-day cycle, I typically see companies using two periods at the end of each month for reassessment. In a monthly cycle, the recommendation is to have a shorter adjustment period every week.

The adjustment period is just a quick check-in on the progress of our initiatives in the current cycle. It's a review of assumptions and a chance to address questions like, "Has anything changed fundamentally within my organization or the market conditions?" An adjustment period is *not* the time to take a deep dive or to do a complete rethink of things; it is an opportunity to ensure that the company stays on course during the cycle.

At the completion of the acceleration cycle, you can reassess and rejudge more thoroughly. This is when we would look at the active roadmap and determine if our zones and initiatives still fit within the scope of the destination we've aligned ourselves toward. Does everything still fit? Does everything still apply? Given the results of this most recent acceleration cycle, are any major changes in order?

In some organizations, whole teams are built and specialized around specific zones within specific cycles. Once the timeframe and scale of required effort and resources are defined, an organization not only knows what it wants to do, but also has a clear target for when and how it must be done.

When we talk about action plans and grids and the three zones of execution, we aren't just telling you to do busywork. We are helping them find their effective initiative. These are methods to enable their ability to keep a degree of focus on long-term goals of consistent and sustainable revenue growth.

TIPS AND TAKEAWAYS

In Chapter 16, we covered the fundamentals of an effective execution—what ultimately differentiates the victorious from the not-so-victorious. To increase the success of your business's execution, you should:

- Identify the game(s) you are playing and avoid playing to the lowest common denominator,
- Step out of your system in order to embrace change, transformation, and winning your unfair share,
- Define your acceleration cycle to ensure consistent and predictable periods of execution and adjustment,
- And achieve more effective execution through the implementation of the three zones: performance, enablement, and transformation.

If everything is a priority, nothing is a priority.

The reason your company is working so damn hard and you're still getting so little juice for the squeeze is that you're trying to do too much too fast. You're trying to progress by leaps and bounds, and you're not taking advantage of the power of consistent iteration and improvement. The former leads to burnout for the people in your company; the latter ensures sustainability. Less is more, and prioritization and focus can be you and your business's superpower.

CHAPTER 17

REVENUE ACCELERATION MINDSET

I LOVE BASEBALL. (HAVE YOU NOTICED THAT YET?) AND SOME OF my favorite baseball stories come from 2016, the year Joe Madden led the Chicago Cubs to their first World Series win in almost a hundred years.

Madden was the sort of team manager who, in the middle of August, started something he called the "let's go back to high school" week for the Chicago Cubs. For those of you who aren't crazy about major league baseball, I'll tell you that pro players will typically get to the stadium somewhere around eleven o'clock to noon for a seven o'clock game and go through training, preparation, batting practice, et cetera for hours. For a week in August, Joe Madden told his players they were not allowed to report to the stadium earlier than five o'clock for a seven o'clock game. The idea was to bring the team morale back to what it's like to play the sport in high school. High school players go to class, get on the bus to go to the game, put on their cleats while they are on the bus, and then go out and play the game.

The whole idea behind the change was to loosen the team up because Joe Madden is a big believer in the idea of taking what you do seriously, but not taking yourself seriously. One of the primary catchphrases Joe Madden used throughout the entire year, as the Cubs left the clubhouse and headed into the dugout at the start of the game, was, "Let's try not to suck today." That phrase captured what I think is a great mindset for anyone or any business seeking outstanding performance, growth, and transformation. It's a mindset that I've followed within my own company.

One of the Navy Seal's primary mantras, especially during the famous hell week (or infamous, depending upon your point of view) is to "embrace the suck." Lean into the difficulty and get comfortable being uncomfortable.

I find one of the biggest challenges people face when driving growth or transformation is that people get focused—even obsessed—with getting it right. But in something as dynamic and complex as business growth and the systems associated with it, there really is no such thing as "right."

Now, don't get me wrong; there are a lot of "wrong" ways to do things. However, the focus on getting it right puts a scathing amount of pressure on everybody involved. In my experience, that pressure creates an environment of fear and scarcity when what's needed is an environment of freedom and testing. Brené Brown, author and podcast host, refers to this necessary testing process as creating the shitty first draft.

For myself, my team, and the companies that we work with, my advice is that rather than aiming to get things right, our goal should be to try to suck a little bit less every day.

WHAT SUCK LESS MEANS

Carol Dweck, author of *Mindset*, coined the terms fixed and growth mindsets.

As an industrial psychologist, Dweck wanted to learn how people dealt with frustration. So she went into elementary schools to observe the behavior of kids, because there's no better place to learn how humans deal with stress than watching kids in elementary school. (And I don't mean that sarcastically.)

During the experiment, they would have kids work on puzzles that would become increasingly difficult. The goal was to see what would happen when the kids went from working on the easy puzzles to the harder ones. When left to their natural devices, how would they respond? She expected they would get frustrated, but Dweck and her team were actually surprised by what they saw.

The kids fell into two groups. One group responded much the way they expected, which is that they were very happy to play with the puzzles when they were easy, but got increasingly frustrated to the point where most of them just quit playing once the puzzles got more difficult.

Unexpectedly, there was another group of kids, about the same size as the first, who became *more* engaged with the puzzles once they became more challenging. It was actually hard to get the children in this second group engaged when the puzzles were easy. Only when presented with a challenge did the play response kick in.

The first group of kids had what Dreck describes as the fixed mindset. They judged themselves by their ability to be right. "I'm good if I'm right, I'm bad if I'm not right." With a fixed mindset, the moment you had to work harder and think more, that was a sign something was wrong. The second group of kids had a growth mindset. People with a growth mindset measured themselves by their effort; it was the struggle that was the play. This underlying phenomenon is also key to making a successful video game. If a game is too easy, people get bored with it and quit. If a game is too hard, people get too frustrated and quit. The trick is to find balance between a task being hard enough to engage, but not so hard that it feels impossible.

Furthermore, Dreck and her team found that people and areas that exhibit growth mindsets have greater resilience. They don't tie themselves to their results or their outcomes. As a result, they learn better. They learn faster and tend to perform at a higher level.

If you're going to be involved in driving growth and transformation, you are going to be in uncomfortable situations regularly. After all, growing a business isn't easy, or else everybody would be a successful business owner. If you don't build a mindset that enables you to be comfortable in challenging environments, you're not going to be able to sustain your business's growth journey.

People tend to live in a "right or wrong," binary world. But right and wrong actually exist on a continuum. There's wrong. There's not wrong. There's not right. And there's right. You certainly want to avoid being totally wrong wherever possible. But it's important to remember there are actually very few places where you have to be totally right. More often than not, just not being wrong is going to be enough. That's part of the idea behind the "try to suck less" mindset. We don't live in a right/wrong world, so let's focus instead on how we get a little bit better every day. How do we reduce the pressure on improvement and write that shitty first draft? That's what matters.

When we hire new people, they're always kind of taken a little bit back the first time I say something like, "Hey, let's suck a little bit less." We've been conditioned from a young age to try to be right as much as possible. So every time we get new people at Imagine, they misinterpret me saying, "suck less," as me saying, "you suck." And nothing could be further from my intent.

Have you ever looked at a horizon? It's a pretty cool thing to look at. But have you ever tried to touch the horizon? You'll find that the more you move towards the horizon, the more the horizon moves away from you. The problem with a "try to be right" mindset is that being right is an illusion. It's a lot like the horizon. That's the problem with thinking, "Hey, if I can just fix this problem the right way, then everything will be fine." But anybody that's been involved in a successful business has learned that the high wire just gets higher. For every problem you solve, three new ones that are a little bit more complex and a little bit more nuanced emerge. When you're focused on being right, it's filled with pressure to not get it wrong.

So, here's how I look at it. You are where you are. People are surprised by how excited I get when we learn that something is broken or that we're really sucking at something. Here's why I get excited. If an area is broken and not functioning at all the way we want it to, the fact that it's not working doesn't change where we are as an organization. It means we've gotten to where we are *despite* the fact that something is broken. If something is broken, I don't see failure; I see opportunity. And it's a lot easier to improve something that's broken than it is to improve something that's already working really well.

Just imagine for a moment that nothing was broken at your business or nothing was ineffective about what you were doing. What would that mean? It would mean that, right now, at this moment in time, things are as good as they're ever going to be. Because if everything's working optimally, how are you going to get any better?

I know that growth is challenging. If it weren't, people like me wouldn't write books about it. But the "suck less" mindset can reduce the fear of challenge. It takes the pressure off and turns the focus onto learning and making progress. That's where the focus should be.

DOWNSTREAM PROBLEMS AND UPSTREAM SOLUTIONS

Most people who are responsible for executing a company strategy feel more like this truck trying to get through the underpass and less like a high-powered business person who's two to three steps ahead of everybody.

The idea of addressing problems when we see them is alluring because it's simple, and everybody wants to keep things simple. What they miss is that simple—the real *simple*, not the buzzword—lives on the opposite side of complexity. This is something I call the "inverse friction principle," which highlights the challenge involved in creating simple things. The inverse friction principle states that the ease or effortlessness of a user's experience has an inverse relationship to the complexity that went into designing the systems that created said experience.

Two great examples of complex designs creating effortless experiences are Amazon and Uber. Have you ever noticed how easy it is to buy anything on Amazon? The ease of using Amazon to buy anything is so prevalent that every online and offline business has had to deal with the rising expectations of people wanting an Amazon experience. But consider what has gone into creating the experience that Amazon has to make everything so easy or effortless for the customer.

The other example I like to use is hailing a ride using the Uber app. I'll never forget the first time I used Uber. I was almost confused because it was so easy; I literally thought I had to be missing something, until two minutes later when the car came up and took me and my guest to our destination. Again, think about what went into creating the Uber app and ride system that made everything so easy or effortless for the users.

To make execution simple, to enable your people to execute with ease and effortlessness, you must strive to solve problems before they happen.

THE INTANGIBLE UPSTREAM

W. Edwards Deming revolutionized manufacturing as we know it with the work that he did with Japanese manufacturers following World War II.

Before Deming, if you were to ever buy a piece of clothing such as a pair of pants or a shirt, more likely than not you'd have to throw away a little piece of paper that had inspector 11 or some other number printed on it. Before Deming and his "total quality management" philosophy, the normal approach to manufacturing was to inspect for defects after the product was made. You would solve problems downstream—as you encountered them.

Then, Deming came along and introduced total quality management, a precursor to the "systems thinking" that we discussed earlier in this book. His philosophy highlighted the fact that problems were more often than not caused by the system, not by the people within the system. So when you treat problems as mistakes in implementation or execution, rather than mistakes in the system, you would get more of those mistakes because the systemic issues were left unaddressed.

According to Deming, every problem should be viewed through the lens of the system and how the system can prevent the mistake. How can we solve the problem before the problem occurs?

Of course, the problem with addressing problems before they become problems in sales, marketing, and customer success is that, upstream, those problems are often invisible, intangible, uncertain, and varying. They require you to think through multiple scenarios and face trade-offs that are often uncomfortable to wrestle with. It feels so much easier, faster, and even more logical to just jump to execution and cross any river when you get to it.

If you're striving to solve problems upstream, I can guarantee you that someone with a degree of power will at some point throw a temper tantrum, asking why you are messing around with theory when you've got work to do. But there's a high cost to such a direct approach. When you don't solve problems upstream, the resulting friction, confusion, and disruption from those problems are pushed into execution.

The latest research from CSO Insights, shared through the HubSpot blog post, "60 Key Sales Statistics That'll Help You Sell Smarter in 2021," shows that salespeople spend less than 33 percent of their time actually selling. Why? Because they have to spend far too much time managing the administrative aspects associated with their jobs and chasing down their manager or someone else to find out how to handle something. What's sad is the very technology that companies have been spending billions of dollars on to eliminate the need to do so much non-productive, low-value work has only increased the amount of non-productive, low-value work that needs to be done. The trend on this data point has been consistently negative for the last 20 years.

The late Peter Drucker, a noted business thought leader and management consultant, said it best: "To sustain or scale growth, you must build the genius into the system." You cannot wait to cross every river when you get to it. The only way to execute at scale is to address the barriers, conflicts, confusions, and ambiguities before they hit the point of execution.

FOUR STEPS TO SOLVING PROBLEMS UPSTREAM

The only way to get more from your resources and inputs is to eliminate the disruption that drags execution. And you do that by solving problems upstream.

"Easier said than done," you might think. Because how do we actually solve problems upstream, before they happen? This is one of the areas where the power of the Revenue Acceleration Framework is critical for success, because the Framework provides the roadmap for the stream. Go-to-market strategy leads to structure, structure leads to approach, approach leads to execution.

Beyond using the Framework as a (well) framework to create upstream solutions and achieve revenue acceleration and growth, you can also increase the number of problems you are able to solve by doing the following four things:

Number one, define your desired outcomes. Begin with the end in mind. What is it that we're trying to achieve? What does success look like?

Number two, do a "what causes success" analysis. When we work with sales organizations that are looking to transform their sales approach, one of the first things we'll do is a "what causes sales" analysis. We'll work to identify the key inflection points and areas that influence the outcomes we're looking for. This enables us to highlight the elements necessary to focus on issues better, to test better, and to learn faster.

Number three, map the processes involved. Abraham Lincoln is credited with saying, "Great communication is not communicating to be understood. It's communicating so that you won't be misunderstood." Too often, people talk about their processes or list them in a spreadsheet. But to understand a process, you have to be able to see it visually. A mapped-out process enables everyone to see things the same way.

We see it happen time and time again, where senior teams or RevOp teams will discuss issues while only using words. It may sound like there's agreement and alignment in the conversation, but everybody walks away with a slight (sometimes tremendous) difference in interpretation of the words said. It's not until we lay out a map that we're really able to achieve alignment around the now clearly identifiable issues that need to be addressed.

Number four, practice hypothesis-driven growth. We're looking for progress, not perfection. So, once we identify an outcome, we establish an idea of what we think will enable us to achieve that outcome. Because we've stated our hypothesis, we can then see how the world works in relation to our current hypothesis, which enables us to set our next hypothesis, which creates a cycle that leads to the progress we're looking for. The objective is not to be right. It's just to suck a little bit less every day.

FIVE BARRIERS TO UPSTREAM PROBLEM-SOLVING

Besides the four steps to creating more effective upstream solutions, you should also be aware of the five potential pitfalls of upstream solutions.

One, upstream solutions often take time to come to fruition. This is why taking a three-zones approach to execution is so important. If you are not looking to solve the problems that are going to impact you 18 months from today, you're going to find growth harder and harder to sustain.

Two, measuring the ROI of problems not happening is very difficult.

Three, there is no glory in preventing problems. No one sits around the conference room table telling the heroic tale of "That one time five years ago when Frank prevented a problem from ever happening." Of course they don't, because the problem never happened.

Four, there's no urgency. Upstream solutions are important, but they're not urgent. Without clear zones of execution, people get caught up in the whirlwind of solving day-to-day problems that are less important but more urgent.

Five, downstream solutions are often tangible, easier to see, and easier to measure. One of the biggest challenges that a strong RevOps organization has is the reduction of problems that seems to invalidate the necessity of the organization. As RevOps gets better at solving problems before they happen, fewer problems happen. People begin to wonder, "Why are we spending so much money on revenue operations when there've been no problems?"

It's important to keep a strong structure in place to circumvent these five barriers which can prevent you from effectively solving upstream.

THE FUNCTION OF FRICTION

As I'm writing this book, I recently got a puppy—Dakota. She's a rambunctious seven-month-old great Pyrenees. This was a decision the family made after we lost our beautiful dog of 12 years, Darby. During Darby's life, she'd had some health issues that proved to be very costly, and, being a firm believer in learning from my own mistakes, when we got Dakota we also got pet insurance.

I went to a company because of a recommendation from a close associate, and I've got to give this company credit; the user experience in completing the application and getting the insurance was far easier than I ever expected it to be. It was even a little bit entertaining. At the end of the application, this company highlighted that I could cut the cost of my pet insurance even more if I bundled it with my homeowner's insurance. They asked if I'd like to get a quote on it, and I figured, "Sure. What the heck. Insurance is insurance. What have I got to lose?"

I got about a third of the way through the application for homeowner's insurance and stopped. Why? Because they were asking for a whole bunch of things that I didn't have access to at the moment. They wanted information on my existing homeowner's policy. They wanted to know what my mortgage balance was—information that most of us don't know off the top of our heads. In theory, I could have gone home, put the stuff together, and come back. But the reality is, I didn't.

What this company did successfully was create a very low-friction experience. The friction was so low that I seamlessly went into applying for another piece of insurance on the spot, but I wasn't ready for that. If I were advising this company, I would've given an option to download a list and have an email sent to customers to pick up their application where they left off. Now, I get what they were trying to do. This insurance company wanted to lower the friction of starting the insurance bundle because they wanted to get me through the door. But this is a perfect example of where the function of friction gets misunderstood.

Lord knows I have spent a good chunk of this book highlighting the negative attributes of friction. And I can certainly vouch for the fact that growth organizations have a much bigger problem with eliminating low-value friction than missing high-value friction. But it is a foundational, fundamental mistake to believe that friction is bad. Even though the legacy thinking about friction is simply to *eliminate it*. The real problem isn't that companies have too much friction. It is that, specifically, they have way too much low-value friction and not enough high-value friction.

If you want to accelerate revenue, you need to change your relationship with friction, and you must view it as the tool that it is. Friction is a tool; it's a tactic. So, instead of asking *if* you should use friction, start asking yourself *how* you want to use it. Not all friction is bad.

Let me give you an example of friction that I'm certain everybody reading this book is happy to have. And that is treads on the tires of cars. The entire purpose of tire treads is to create friction; friction creates traction. If the treads begin to wear down and disappear, it's time for you to change your tires. You see, if your tires didn't have treads, your car would spin out of control the moment they encountered any bit of water. This is why, if you've ever watched a NASCAR race, the moment the first drop of rain hits the track, all the cars go in to change their tires.

Stop for a moment and think about the highest value, most memorable experience that you've ever had, whether it was commercial or interpersonal. Every single one of those events is an example of friction. All value comes from friction. If there wasn't any friction associated with the experience, you wouldn't remember that the experience happened. Then, by definition, it wouldn't be memorable. If it doesn't register, then it can't be one of the greatest, most memorable experiences you've ever had.

The mistake of eliminating friction without managing friction contributes heavily to commoditizing businesses today. When the user experience is so frictionless, it becomes featureless. They can't tell the meaningful difference between one company and another.

So, what is friction in the context of RevOps? Whenever you're designing or drafting any kind of experience, whenever you're trying to achieve any type of outcome, you need to understand that you really have only two tools at your disposal; in other words, two types of pressure. The one that we're most familiar with and we spend the most time dealing with is promoting pressure. You want the people in your company to do something, so you draft the campaign. You create posters. You introduce incentives. These are all examples of promoting pressures.

The second type is inhibiting pressure, and friction is one major type of inhibiting pressure. While promoting pressures incentivizes people, inhibiting pressures does the opposite; they make it harder for customers to deviate from the path you want them to take.

As an example, if you wanted to increase participation in a retirement program, what would you do? Well, using promoting pressures, you could add a reminder to contribute to their 401(k) in the email confirming their direct deposit receipt. You might introduce a match; if they give money, you'll match some of it to make the retirement program worth the participation. These are promoting pressures.

In contrast, one of the most successful efforts using inhibiting pressure to increase contributions to retirement programs was to flip participation in the program on its head. Rather than making people sign up to participate in the 401(k), people had to "sign up" to opt out of the 401(k). In these cases, the sign-up process became an inhibiting pressure.

That whole flip from opt-in to opt-out for 401(k)'s demonstrates one of the most famous concepts in behavioral science—people are creatures of least resistance. One of the biggest challenges you'll face when you're trying to influence the behaviors of people, both internally and externally, is that if it's easier *not* to do something than to do it, people aren't likely to do it. The limitations to the usual approach that people take in their go-to-market efforts is that they only focus on promoting pressure—what they want people to do—as opposed to what they don't want people to do.

Friction, on the other hand, can be as powerful of a tool as inhibiting pressure. As you craft experiences, you'll want to use high-value friction as a tool to nudge the direction that people go in. Friction also slows things down. In sales processes and go-to-market processes, if you want someone to change the course or speed that they're on, they will have to slow down at some point and think. Many years ago, we learned that a telltale sign that someone would buy from us was if they stopped and considered their existing situation and came to the conclusion that change wasn't only beneficial, but necessary. If they had the chance to slow down and think, oftentimes they had the chance to realize they needed to change. But when you only eliminate friction, all you'll do is accelerate the path that somebody is on. You don't give them the opportunity to think.

Once we realized the importance of eliminating *and* managing friction, we began to add purposeful points of friction designed to slow people down to consider what needed changing. Did we lose some opportunities because there were some people who wanted us to just send 'em a proposal? I'm sure we did. But our growth rate increased. Our margins increased. Our average sale value increased, and our satisfaction and lifetime values increased as well.

FOUR STEPS TO CONDUCTING A FRICTION AUDIT

1. Map the journey or journeys that your customers go through when buying from you.
2. Identify the high-impact inflection points. What are the critical few points in that journey that really determine the path and speed that they're going to follow?
3. Identify where people need to speed up. Where do people get bogged down at points of low value? Eliminate friction in those areas.
4. Identify where people need to slow down. Where do they need to think? Add high-value friction to those places.

Remember, where there's no friction, there's no value. You want friction where you want it, and you don't want it where you don't. The key to being successful with friction is to be purposeful.

THINK PROBABILISTICALLY

February 1, 2015, the New England Patriots were leading the Seattle Seahawks 28 to 24.

There were 24 seconds left in the game. The Seahawks had the ball on the Patriots' one yard line, one second down. The Seahawks had no timeouts and one of the league's top rushers, Marshawn Lynch, in the backfield. Everybody knew the play that would be called. Russell Wilson was going to hand the ball off to Marshawn Lynch, and every Patriots fan that I knew was convinced this would be the end. The Patriots were going to lose the Super Bowl.

But that's not what happened. In what has been dubbed by many to be among the worst play calls in the history of football, if not all of professional sports, Pete Carroll called for a pass. Seahawks fans and Patriots haters everywhere gasped, "What were you thinking?"

That pass was intercepted by the Patriots' Malcolm Butler.

According to author, consultant, and winner of the 2004 World Series of Poker tournament of champions, Annie Duke, the response to that worst play call in the history of play calls is a great example of resulting, which is a common poker term for the human tendency to judge the quality of the decisions we make by the outcomes of those decisions.

Here's a question that not enough people consider: Was the call that Carroll made a bad one?

Unquestionably, if we're going to judge Pete Carroll's choice by the outcome of the game, it was among the worst that could ever happen. But people who replayed that moment over and over, roasting Carroll for his decision, were considering only one of the multiple scenarios that could have happened. Wilson could have handed off the ball to Marshawn Lynch, and Marshawn Lynch could have run it in for a touchdown. That was what everyone thinks would've happened.

However...the handoff could have been bad, and the ball could have been fumbled. Marshawn Lynch could have gotten hit after receiving the handoff and fumbled. Marshawn Lynch could have been tackled for no gain or a loss, and with no timeouts left, the clock would've continued to tick. The Seahawks could have been called for a holding penalty or some other penalty and be pushed back from the one-yard line.

Now, let me tell you something interesting about that 2014 season. Less than 1 percent of passes from the one-yard line ended in anything other than a reception for a touchdown or an incomplete pass. So if you're Pete Carroll and you're considering what could happen, making the decision to pass the ball represents a 99 percent probability that you'll achieve the same result that everyone expected from handing the ball off the Lynch, or you would at least have had the opportunity to run another play with about 15 seconds remaining. And if you were Carroll in 2014, you might've also considered that no passes resulted in an interception from the one-yard line that year. Butler's was the first.

It's up to anybody's judgment as to whether that call was a good one or not. But I remain convinced that one of the reasons Pete Carroll has maintained a successful career as a head coach of a national football league team is because, while fans think deterministically, Pete Carroll thinks probabilistically.

DETERMINISTIC VS. PROBABILISTIC THINKING

Deterministic thinking believes in one of two outcomes. We will score a touchdown. We won't score a touchdown. Deterministic thinking is binary thinking. Right or wrong. Probabilistic thinking realizes that there's an infinite number of possibilities between zero and one.

What leads to our outcomes? There are only two things that determine the outcomes for any individual or any business. Luck and the quality of the decisions that we make. We have no control over luck. The only thing we have control over is decision quality, and to make better decisions, we need to understand that important outcomes are rarely certain. One of the great human weaknesses is our abject desire for certainty. As the French philosopher Voltaire wrote, "Uncertainty is an uncomfortable position, but certainty is an absurd one." This is a truth that extends beyond business, football, and philosophy.

Stop for a moment and imagine a scenario where you've got plans for the weekend. You're going to be outside; maybe you're having a picnic, maybe you're golfing. You turn on the weather forecast, and it says there's a 70 percent chance of rain. What do you do? If you're like most people, you cancel your plans or you move them inside.

Then, Saturday comes around, and it doesn't rain. How do you react? Again, if you're like most people, you're calling the weather forecaster all sorts of names that I won't be saying in this book. Because when you hear there's a 70 percent chance of rain, you walk away thinking it's going to rain. But what does 70 percent really mean? It means that seven out of ten times, the expected outcome is rain. But three out of ten times, it's not going to rain.

You might yell up at the clear blue skies, "How can weather people get it so wrong?!" But did they get it wrong?

The inability to understand probabilities is one of the major causes of bad decisions in business. In my experience, especially in the world of sales and marketing, certainty begins to emerge at about a 33 percent probability. If the decision cycle is more than a week out, the actual win percentage is roughly 35 percent. We've looked at opportunities that meet certain criteria where organizations have forecasted sales opportunities into what's called "commits." They begin to operate under the idea of "We are *going* to win this one!"

The reason we tend to think in terms of certainty, even when things are clearly uncertain, is because when we predict outcomes we don't take into consideration the things that are going to happen outside of our control. For example, even as I write this book, there's a major sea change in the macroeconomic environment of the business world we're operating in. Budgets are changing within a lot of organizations, and opportunities are easily lost today because of such budget reconfigurations. It's all down to luck. Had the opportunities presented themselves 90 days earlier than they did, the budget reconfigurations might never have happened.

As we start thinking about those "commits" and developing certainty over the probabilities of outcomes, we mistakenly discount the things that we have little or no control over. This leads to unpredictable outcomes which cause us to overreact to the positive when things are good and overreact to the negative when things are bad.

So, one of the simplest ways to carve out an execution advantage for you over your competitors is to think probabilistically, not deterministically.

POKER IS THE BETTER METAPHOR

I am sick and tired of people saying, "Play chess, not [insert name of whatever other game]." Chess is a horrible metaphor for business and life. You see, chess contains no hidden information, and there's very little luck. The pieces are all there for everybody to see. Nobody has to guess about anything. If you lose at a game of chess, it must be because there were better moves that you didn't make or didn't see. In the game of chess, the best player always wins, unless the best player makes a mistake.

Chess is a game of managing and computing perfect information, but business and life is not a game of perfect information. What's more, the information in the game of business and life is always changing.

I've mentioned many times in this book about the importance of making decisions and choices, and what I want you to understand is that every decision you make is a bet on the future. I always laugh when an entrepreneurial associate of mine says something along the lines of "well, *if* I were a betting man or woman…" because, in fact, they *are* a betting person. The decision to start a business was a bet. The decision to take a job was a bet. The decision to implement anything is a bet on future outcomes. And when you're crafting your strategy to go to market, to implement a marketing campaign, to win a piece of business, you will never have all of the information you need to know if you made the "right" decision or not.

The old phrase, "hindsight is 20/20" also isn't true, because anything that you would've done differently earlier in the process would've changed everything else that was happening. The situation that you find yourself in now will never be the exact same one that you find yourself in again. That's why poker is a far better metaphor for business and life.

Poker is a game where you must manage and make decisions without having access to everything that matters. It's a game where you can play the right hand and lose. You can play the game well, you can be the better player overall, and still lose. On the bright side, you can play a hand badly and win.

Guy Hanson, winner of three World Poker Tour titles, was once asked by a reporter what role luck played in poker. He responded that in any given session, it probably accounted for about 90 percent of his outcomes. Over a month, he guessed it was about 10 to 15 percent. And over a year, it was down to around 2 to 5 percent. Over time, the better player will win more money, so long as they stick to a better decision process. The same is true when you go to market.

In both poker and business, there are rules; but following those rules doesn't automatically make you a great player. In both games, consistent and long-term success is a mix of luck and great decision-making. Imagine if you didn't know that a 2–7 offsuit hand was a bad hand (probably the worst hand) to start with in Texas Hold'em. Chances are, any single game you won would be a matter of luck. But when you know the rules well, you raise your chances of being a pretty good poker player. If you have the mental fortitude to stick to the rules, you'll be a good poker player. And it's only when you know when and how to break those rules that you have the opportunity to become a great poker player.

As I began to dig into the game of poker, one of the most interesting things I learned is that the best players out there folded far more frequently than the average poker players do. They fold early and they fold in the middle more frequently than other players. What great poker players know is that every time a card gets dealt, every round, the situation changes. The decisions that were made or what went into those decisions in a previous round should not dictate the decisions that are made in a current round. This is why the best poker players are selective in the hands that they play. Far too often, people get stuck in the sunk cost fallacy, where they let the previous decisions they've made dictate the decisions that they continue to make.

My favorite game of poker as a metaphor for go to market is Texas Hold'em. In Texas Hold'em, you go through five rounds. The first round is called the preflop. Everybody is dealt two cards, face down. Nobody knows what those two cards are. The next round is called the flop, where the first three out of five common cards are turned over in the center of the table. Next is the turn, when the fourth common card is turned over. Then the river, which is the fifth common card. After each round with the cards is a round of betting. In Texas Hold'em, your two cards plus the three best common cards determine your hand that's played, and whoever is the last person remaining wins the pot. If more than one person stays, it comes to what's called the showdown; whoever has the best hand of the remaining players wins. So, you have five rounds where the context of the game you're playing is changing. Managing a dynamic process where things are constantly changing and being able to keep your head and stay focused are key to success in poker. And they're obviously key to success in business.

Before I finish with this metaphor, there are some very important differences between poker and business that I do need to point out. The first one is that, at the end of the day, poker is either a zero sum or negative sum game. If you're playing with your buddies, it's a zero sum game because the amount that people win is going to be equal to the amount that other people lose. If you play at a casino, it's a negative sum game because you've got to cover what's called the "rake," which goes to the casino. But in the game of revenue growth and acceleration, you're playing an additive game, which represents an important difference in the types of outcomes you're seeking from a business game vs. a poker game.

This brings me to the second difference between poker and business. In poker, you only have opponents. In business, it's important to keep in mind that you are not playing *against* your customers. When I talk about the rounds in poker, it's also a metaphor of the thought and decision process that goes into each game, where poker's process is a win/lose, but your revenue growth process needs to be win/win.

Finally, poker has a set number of rounds. In Texas Hold'em, there's five rounds. Nothing you do would change the number of rounds and the two cards you and the other players are dealt in the game. You get what you get, and you must play your hand or fold. That's entirely different in the game of business and life. One of the biggest missed opportunities that I see in selling is when people stick so closely to the standard process that they forget they have the option to change the number of rounds in the process and even change the metaphorical cards that people are playing. If you can change how somebody thinks about the issue that they're dealing with, you can turn a weak hand into a strong hand for yourself and a strong hand into a weak hand for your competitors.

FOCUS IS YOUR SUPERPOWER

If you've gotten to this point of the book, I hope that one of the key takeaways you've picked up is this:

While the dominant thinking about growing a business is about more and more and more, the path that leads to better outcomes is to do less with more.

It's really easy in the world of business to get lost in all that you have to do, but it's important to keep in mind that you only have a very limited amount of time to do what needs to get done. So, make sure that you're using the time effectively. When I'm working with sales teams or coaching organizations, one of my favorite things to do is talk about how little time we have in a year.

Think about your typical year, which has 365 days. That's a lot of days, but when you take out weekends and 11 federally mandated holidays, you're left with just 250 days. Now take out two weeks of vacation. (I hope you're taking more than that. But if not, then I hope you're getting *at least* two weeks of vacation.) This leaves 240 weekdays to actually do work. But realize you don't get to spend all of your days doing work. Depending upon what your role is and what the situation is, most studies show that people spend only 30 to 50 percent of their time actually doing the work that needs to get done. So, think of all the administrative aspects that you have to take care of. If you're lucky, you get about 120 days to do all of the things that you were planning out for a 365-day year.

How are you going to use your days?

Realize that humans and organizations all have three fundamental resources. The first two, what I refer to as time and effort, are really the energy that people bring to bear. Why do companies hire more people? To generate a greater capacity of time and effort. The third resource is money. Typically, energy and money work in tandem. The more money you have, the more time and effort you can buy, or the more you can invest in things that enable you to do more with the time and effort that you have.

It doesn't matter what point you're at, business-wise. You could be the person that just started your business today, working from your kitchen table. You could have a full-time job and very limited resources to spare. You could already be a decision-maker for one of the largest companies in the world. But at the end of the day, you will always have limited time, effort, and money.

So how do you get more from the time, effort, and money than you already have? (Say it with me now: How do you get more juice for the squeeze?) This is where I discovered the superpower that every human has, a power that is probably greater than any other tool or resource that we use and even better than AI or any other technology we've invented.

Our superpower is focus.

The key to driving success, the formula that I've been able to create to maximize the probability of success for any individual organization, comes down to a simple equation of focus, where your focus times the limited resources that you have, allocated to the best opportunities to use those resources for, equals the level of success that you'll experience.

Of course, this superpower is counterintuitive to what we've been told from a young age. "Don't put all your eggs in one basket," and "Always spread your bets." Certainly, I'm not suggesting that you should only focus on focus. Another facet to the counterintuitive nature of execution is that we tend to think, "If I can only do more, I have a better chance of accomplishing what I want to accomplish."

In reality, the more that you do, the more likely you'll experience average outcomes at best. The key to generating the type of success that I assume you're looking for (by mere fact that you're reading this book and not some book called *Revenue Stagnation: A Proven Roadmap to Staying Average*) comes from choosing fewer opportunities.

Success comes from an ability to focus more of what you're doing on the fewer things that have a chance to have the biggest impact. In other words, with greater focus you can allocate more resources to your best opportunities.

TIPS AND TAKEAWAYS

In Chapter 17, we reviewed the different facets of an effective revenue acceleration mindset. To create this mindset for yourself and the people in your business, you should:

- Try to suck less and progress instead of fixating on how to be right,
- Treat friction as a tool that gives you greater control over your growth and transformation journey,
- And avoid discounting the factors that create uncertainty of outcomes and instead embrace probabilistic thinking.

Your business's successful execution of the Revenue Acceleration Framework begins with the right mindset. While I will tell you, "Try to suck less," remember that I don't mean to say, "You suck." Because you don't. Rather, you should try to embrace the uncertainty of writing your shitty first draft and be willing to be "not right" in an effort to make real progress.

Understand that, with the proper mindset and willingness to commit to the RevOps process, you *can* achieve more. You can get more juice for the squeeze.

CHAPTER 18

SUCCEEDING WITH REVOPS

ABOUT FIVE YEARS AGO, WE STARTED FOCUSING ON AND TALKING about revenue operations.

About two and a half years ago, we started noticing that many others were starting to talk about revenue operations too.

Today, it feels like you can't get away from people talking about RevOps.

I was initially very excited to see the concept that I thought might take several years to enter mainstream business conversations become so popular so soon. Unfortunately, the popularity of RevOps reflected its trend toward the "magic pill, silver bullet" area of business ideas, with people claiming all you need to do is implement revenue operations; everything else will take care of itself.

I've long evangelized the belief that long-term success is more about the plumbing and structure that enable execution than it is about the great strategies that tend to get the credit. For this reason, I'm all in on the rising popularity of revenue operations. However, there's a common problem that we've seen with trends like this that get so hot. They devolve into buzzwords and empty gestures promising quick fixes and magic elixirs. They quickly move up the hype cycle only to ultimately disappoint because people fail to have the right expectations or lack commitment to the actions necessary to succeed with RevOps.

Implementing revenue operations is a core strategic decision. Succeeding with revenue operations requires deep understanding about the underlying drivers of success for your business, attention, and specific skills.

WHAT MAKES SUCCESS

From as early as I can remember, I've been fascinated by the nature of human success. In many ways, I feel like everything that I've done in my career has been in pursuit of one question that I've thought about my entire life:

Why do some people do things that work, and others, who seem equally capable and equally talented, don't?

The question has manifested itself in a lot of different ways. Why do people make the decisions that they make? How do people respond to different stimuli? How do they behave in periods of risk? How do they behave when they're comfortable? I think my fascination comes from what I will candidly refer to as my strategic laziness. I've never been one of those people who's been about hustle, hustle, hustle. I've always wanted to know how I can get more juice for the squeeze. I'm interested in the path that enables me to work a little bit less hard, a little bit less intensively than others, and generate greater outcomes. Along the way, I've discovered that A, there are no shortcuts and B, the line between success and failure of RevOps comes down to small, almost imperceptible differences that are carried out consistently over time.

When I started in business, I believed in the power of good ideas. I wanted to outthink my competition, and that brought me to the world of strategy. I wanted to believe that if you could come up with a better idea and have a little bit better strategy, that would make the difference. But I soon learned good ideas and good strategies aren't nearly as rare as I thought they were, and they aren't what make the real difference. In some ways, I'd say I still believe in the value of good ideas, though that belief has become more realistic over the years.

When I coached college baseball, I also learned that the root of the difference of success wasn't just reflected in business. It was reflected in athletics, too. I had the opportunity to coach many baseball players who had every bit of talent that others who became far more famous and far more successful had. But the outcomes weren't just about luck. As I've had the opportunity to talk to others, basically every performance discipline in the world comes down to the same small, almost imperceptible differences in the systems, skills, and disciplines between those who achieve the outcomes that we all dream about...and those who could never quite kick it into gear.

There comes a point in time in everybody's life, no matter how good they are at anything, where they're going to come into the company of others who are almost as good, if not a little bit better. That's when those habits, disciplines, and consistencies truly pay off.

THE UNDENIABLE IMPORTANCE OF BUSINESS ACUMEN

Twenty years ago, I was running a two-day training program for an emerging group of salespeople, where someone asked me, "What's your definition of a great salesperson?"

And I said, "A great salesperson is one who can sell when there's nothing to buy."

Since that day, I've had the ability to refine my definition, and what I would tell you today is this: The difference between a great salesperson and a not-so-great salesperson is that the great salesperson is a business person who sells. They're a business person first, salesperson second. The difference between a great marketer and a not-so-great marketer is that the great marketer is a business person who markets. There's a crucial discipline and talent and skill when it comes to business, and it's encapsulated in the term "business acumen."

If you want to know what you can do, individually or organizationally, that will have the greatest impact on your business's ability to execute and grow, my answer would be to invest in developing business acumen, because the people who have it have a great advantage.

I can tell you that overall there's less business acumen today than there was 10, 20, 30 years ago. As we've gotten more and more "advanced," we've broken things down to their corresponding components and specializations, and we've become far more efficient and sophisticated than we've ever been. But with more and more specialization, there are fewer and fewer people who can really understand the whole. See, businesses are complex ecosystems. Just as you wouldn't go to a doctor that only understood their discipline and didn't understand anything else about how your body worked, you need to think the same way when it comes to how you lead the decisions your business is making.

Today, more than ever before, individuals who possess business acumen have a tremendous advantage over those that don't. This is especially true in sales, marketing, and the emerging discipline of RevOps. What's happening in business today is that we're copying examples of success, not creating our own path to success. Those that can create their path of success will gain greater velocity toward their growth and revenue objectives than those who are stuck repeating the status quo.

So, what is business acumen? Business acumen is the ability to intuitively grasp the performance drivers for your or someone else's business. It is the ability to clearly explain how your processes, methodologies, products, or services will drive results and outcomes. It's an "ROI on the fly" conversation. It's an equal mixture of business understanding, asking the right questions, and pouncing on a great opportunity when it presents itself.

When your team possesses business acumen, you experience greater growth, bigger margins, and a much stronger competitive position. When you don't have it, then the only long-term future for your business is competition, commoditization, and compressed margins.

HOW TO TALK TO A CEO ABOUT REVENUE OPERATIONS

A few common statements I get are, "Hey, Doug! I love your ideas. Unfortunately, that's not how the business I'm employed at works," or

"I'd love to add RevOps, but my CEO and the higher ups don't think that way," and "How do I introduce RevOps to my CEO?"

When I'm asked those questions, typically the first thing that I'll advise them to do is notice how they framed the questions. They see the situation as, "I'd love to *add* RevOps, but…" That right there is the beginning of a bad path to introduce the concept to your CEO, your board, or anybody else. Whether or not you realize it or have a department for it, RevOps already exists. It's there; it's just not purposeful.

If you're at the point where you feel that RevOps needs more purposeful attention in your organization, your job is not to add it but to highlight, compare, and contrast how the organization is managing RevOps today versus how it could be managing RevOps to succeed.

One of the common mistakes that gets made when people talk to upper levels of management about functions or approaches like RevOps is there's a tendency for people to focus too much on the process rather than the outcomes that revenue operations can impact. There's a tendency to overplay the negative. While the process is important, it's not the way that CEOs and upper management types typically see things; they want numbers and results.

The way to introduce an idea like revenue operations to a CEO that's not already embracing it is to use the Framework and focus on its positive outcomes. What are we trying to achieve? What are we already achieving? Where's the gap? If you can't identify a gap that matters, it is unlikely that any real change is going to take place even if RevOps is implemented.

Identify the key metrics that are going to be impacted by whatever approach you are suggesting. Be sure to prioritize. Far too often, things like revenue operations are presented as an "all or nothing" choice. However, we've discussed that there are zones of execution that can help prioritize and visualize the implementation of RevOps for an organization.

Establish a place to start. Demonstrate what's going to come from that starting point and iterate from there. The key to building a strong RevOps function, whether you've got a motivated CEO or not, is the momentum that's going to come from an iterative approach. Trying to win over somebody who's resistant to the Framework without highlighting the inherent iterative approach would be a mistake.

And remember: Speak their language. Far too often, we revenue operations proponents try to get senior managers to understand revenue operations, rather than demonstrating first our understanding of what matters to the business and how the proposed approach could achieve those objectives.

Whether you're working to initiate a formal function, or you're part of an ongoing RevOps team, you've got to stay focused on what matters in order to keep a seat at the proverbial table.

WHEN'S THE RIGHT TIME TO IMPLEMENT REVOPS?

This is another question I get asked regularly and constantly. And my answer is, "You already have."

Whether you're aware of it or not, revenue operations is the underlying element of the structures, processes, methodologies of the organization. So the question isn't really when is the right time to implement RevOps, but rather when is the right time to *formally* implement and focus on the discipline? When is the right time to make RevOps a core component of somebody's job description?

As I'm writing this book, revenue operations is probably the hottest topic and the fastest growing role in business. If it's not at the peak of its hype cycle, it's got to be getting pretty close. And, as is true with most relatively new ideas that are ramping up to the peak of their popularity, there are a number of people who talk of revenue operations as though it were some magic pill. "Here, take two revenue operations twice a day and go out and experience massive growth."

Many will say the right time to focus on revenue operations is right away. Now, I will share with you that, of the people who say "right away," just about all of them sell some form of revenue operations product or service. You'll notice, throughout this book, I am not suggesting that revenue operations should be the first, second, or third focus of any business. Because the greatest benefits from an investment in RevOps is going to come when you're moving from being a good business to a great business.

Revenue operations is a good to great discipline. It's a good to great focus. Will effective RevOps help a business that's in trouble? Yes, it will. But when businesses are in trouble, and as businesses are only ramping up to that point where they're going to be able to grow effectively and scale, you'll only experience a small portion of the return on the investment in revenue operations.

The truth is, as we're looking to grow our business, there's two categories of plays that we can run. The first category is increased force. Do more, do it better. The second category is to reduce low-value friction. Revenue operations is in the friction category of plays. Unquestionably, there comes a point in every successful business's experience where a focus on reducing friction provides a greater return than a focus on increasing force. But that only happens when force has gotten to a point of critical mass.

So if you're asking the question, "Should I hire my first salesperson or hire RevOps?" It's a pretty simple and easy question for 99 percent of organizations that I've come across, and that's to hire the salesperson. RevOps manages chaos. But if you're a company of seven people, how much chaos can you have? More importantly, how much economic impact can you receive by reducing the chaos of seven people?

It would be easy if I could tell you revenue operations should be introduced at the point that you have X number of people. Unfortunately, that answer isn't so simple. Every business has their issues. There are different elements and different contexts which will determine when the most effective time for focused RevOps will be.

Revenue operations is at its best when it provides a balance to a company that is moving fast. At the beginning of this book, you learned about the difference between speed and velocity. When a company is moving faster and faster, and it's beginning to see diminishing returns from increased speed, that's the indication to focus on implementing RevOps. It's when you start putting that effort into doing more and it's no longer translating into greater velocity that you should focus on revenue operations. That is the moment when it will emerge as a high-impact, high-value discipline for a company.

THE COMMON MISTAKES OF REVOPS

Revenue operations is such an interesting discipline. I love it. My company's been focused on it for more than three years, from when it was still an emerging term in business. When done right, there's nothing that brings the disciplines and the Framework of business together more powerfully than RevOps. There's nothing quite as beautiful as RevOps gone right, though there's probably nothing worse than when RevOps goes wrong.

I learned a long time ago that every strength is a seed of weakness, and every weakness is a seed of strength, and one of the biggest challenges you have when focusing on RevOps is it's very easy to get overly focused on the idea that there is a single "right way" to do it. Over the years, I've observed five additional mistakes that get made repeatedly, and the first mistake when implementing RevOps is **losing the plot**.

The plot is the "why" of doing something, and it's really easy to lose that why. In television, when a story loses the plot, it's called "jumping the shark." Despite how young revenue operations is as a concept, I am seeing RevOps teams left and right jumping the shark. Remember that the keyword in revenue operations is revenue, not operations. The reason for the RevOps role is to create greater revenue velocity, and the place where revenue operations loses its plot is when the focus is on efficiency or process compliance.

Before you know it, RevOps becomes a reason that low-value friction increases, which places a drag on people's ability to execute and an organization's ability to grow. So, keep the focus on accelerating revenue velocity rather than optimizing the process for the sake of optimization.

The second mistake is **having champagne taste on a beer budget**. When I was young and all my money came from an allowance, my mom used to tell me jokingly that I had champagne taste on a beer budget. I see the same type of thing happen when it comes to RevOps. People have great visions of what they want it to do, but they lack the tolerance to actually embrace what would be needed to achieve that level of outcome.

When Imagine works with clients, we talk about five levels of revenue operations with a key differentiation between tactical revenue operations and strategic revenue operations. In markets with turbulence, when there's a lot of change and confusion, it's very easy to get excited about the opportunities of doing things differently. But if you announce and embrace that difference without being fully embedded in the new strategy or approach, then you'll experience virtually no impact in the best of circumstances. In the worst circumstances, you'll actually weaken your business.

The third major mistake that gets made is **failing to use friction effectively**. Remember, friction is a tool. If we didn't have friction, we wouldn't be driving cars. Too often, we talk about the idea of eliminating friction and being frictionless without realizing or accepting that the real goal is not to eliminate friction. It's to gain more effective traction.

The fourth mistake is **fixating on fixes**. The primary job of tactical RevOps is to fix what's broken. But sometimes we focus so much on fixing what's broken that we miss how the fix is more damaging than the problem ever was. Just as under solving a problem can be an issue, over solving can do just as much damage. If you're trying to fix everything, you're not going to be able to fix anything.

And the fifth mistake is **turning RevOps into the department of sales prevention**. The purpose of RevOps is to make it easier and more effective for the organization to generate more revenue. In RevOps, your job is to make it easier for the sales team to generate strong sales and to increase the average lifetime for the customer. Your job is not to make sure that the CRM is implemented in accordance with its operations manual. While your job may sometimes require you to say no, it is far more important for you to look beyond the no and find the path that enables the team to run with higher efficacy, getting more juice for the squeeze.

TIPS AND TAKEAWAYS

In Chapter 18, we discussed the importance of revenue operations in the face of diminishing business returns. To succeed with RevOps, you must:

- Avoid falling for the hype and treating RevOps as a magic cure-all for every problem.
- Develop business acumen within your organization to gain a greater advantage in execution and growth.
- And remember that while RevOps can create a greater velocity toward success, it is not a linear discipline and there is no one "right way" to implement it.

Revenue operations is a living, breathing discipline. It is complex and powerful and, when done well and implemented at a pivotal point in your business's development, it can generate tremendous advantages and returns.

As a decision-maker, you are at the forefront of a fast-changing business world, and your role in that world is to enable your people in sales, marketing, and customer success to do more, to do better, and to do it with less effort. If your objective is growth and revenue acceleration, then you must be prepared to implement RevOps as a part of your business's framework.

CONCLUSION

CIRCLE INDUSTRIAL IS A VERY SUCCESSFUL INDUSTRIAL SERVICES company formed by a private equity company that had brought several smaller companies together. They were growing, but the legacy areas of the business were responsible for the growth rather than the strategic areas that were the primary basis for the acquisitions. All together, they had more than 50 sales reps selling in multiple verticals, each speaking a slightly different language and describing a slightly different value proposition. They soon realized that they were creating confusion in the market rather than leadership, so they reached out to us to work on tightening and improving their go-to-market messaging and unlocking the latent value which they knew existed beneath all the confusion.

Roughly three years later, Circle Industrial is a fundamentally different company. They're still doing the same activities they did three years ago, yet revenue is growing at faster rates and profits are growing at a faster rate than revenue. Their revenue per rep is increasing. Their markets are clearly defined with strong segmentation and messaging. Having grown to more than a hundred sales reps, they've got over 90 percent adoption for their overall strategy. They have greater insight into their business, and they are reengaging in acquisitions with assimilation times down from two years to somewhere between three to six months. With new acquisitions, they're seeing positive revenue and margin growth after one year where previously these numbers were negative. It is no exaggeration to say that Circle Industrial has experienced a complete transformation.

The interesting thing is this: From the very beginning, they weren't set out to transform anything. They sought only to clarify their go-to-market message, and things quickly unfolded from there.

THE INEVITABLE CHANGE

One of my favorite annual exercises as a decision-maker is looking back on the work that I and Imagine were doing a year ago, three years ago, five years ago, and so on. I've come to learn that this retrospective has proven, time and time again, the importance of meaningful change even within my own company. What were we saying, what were we sharing, and what were we doing? If I'm not at least a bit shocked (and quite a bit embarrassed) by what we were doing in the past, it's highly unlikely that we've had a good year.

If someone were to ask me what this book is about, fundamentally, beneath the descriptions of RevOps and frameworks and games, I would say that this book is about decision-making.

While change is inevitable, great change is purposeful. Regardless of what you do or what you want, your business is going to change because of those decisions and actions and adjustments that you and your people make on a daily basis. That's why change can be such a scary thing for us, because making decisions is scary.

Transformation is a big word, and it brings on big feelings, but it's actually achieved through small, simple decisions and actions. The reason that those small decisions can be so scary is because only once they're made is it easy to see what went wrong. And that fear of consequential change is the barrier that prevents a business from achieving even a fraction of the vast, unimaginable potential and opportunities just beyond its reach.

STANDING IN YOUR ARENA

Every month, during the all-hands meeting, we hold one of my favorite rituals at Imagine. Someone will recite the poem, "Man in the Arena."

> It is not the critic who counts; not the man who points out how the strong man stumbles, or where the doer of deeds could have done them better. **The credit belongs to the man who is actually in the arena,** whose face is marred by dust and sweat and blood; who strives valiantly; who errs, who comes short again and again, because **there is no effort without error** and shortcoming; but who does actually strive to do the deeds; who knows great enthusiasms, the great devotions; who spends himself in a worthy cause; who at the best knows in the end the triumph of high achievement, and who at the worst, if he fails, at least fails while daring greatly, **so that his place shall never be with those cold and timid souls who neither know victory nor defeat.**

I was at a Nationals game a few years ago, where the manager Davey Martinez was getting roasted in the stadium and on Twitter for a decision he'd made. While the vast majority of people who were roasting him didn't know shit about baseball, some of the critics did. And in that moment I had a spike of empathy. I know how hard it is to be the one who makes the types of decisions that have a large and direct impact on the success of others.

If I could go back and talk to anybody who was roasting Dave Martinez that day, I wonder how many of those people would tell me, honestly, that they could make the types of decisions that Martinez had to make, day after day after day. When's the last time that they or you or I have made a decision that was going to impact the livelihood of tens of hundreds of people, while standing before 40,000 onlookers who were going to judge our every decision after the fact?

No matter which team ultimately wins the game, the championships, or the Super Bowl, I still have tremendous respect for the Davey Martinezes, Pete Carrolls, Ryan Lynches, and Mike Donnellys of the world who put their butts on the line and make decisions every day.

Because I know 99 percent of the people who criticize the decisions made, if put under the same pressures, stakes, and time constraints, wouldn't have been able to make a decision at all.

THE STAKES OF DECISION-MAKING

It's easy to make decisions from the sidelines, where the "decision" has no impact on the results. But when something is at stake, there is not just something to win, but also something to lose, and loss is a risk that not everybody can handle. Once there are stakes, even the most experienced people can fumble; anyone who's put money down on a side bet would know this to be true.

Let's say, for example, you and a friend are golfing. Your friend has a gimme putt, and to make it fun, you bet them 50 bucks that they aren't going to make the putt. And your friend might say, "You're nuts. Of course I'm going to make that putt."

But with 50 bucks on the line, the stakes have changed. The pressure hits. More often than not, the putt is missed.

In the years that I was coaching college baseball, I was the bench coach. Part of my job was to regularly consider the situation and what decisions we should be making. I was always in a position to advise the head coach, the manager of the team, during the games and to work on debriefing the decisions that we made after the games.

But one time, during a game that was going to determine whether we would get a bye in the playoffs or not, our manager unexpectedly got ejected. Without prior notice, I was in a position coaching third base in the bottom of the eighth inning, down by two runs, with runners on first and third with one out. And it was solely my job to decide what play we were going to run and to relay the signals. I'd done this more times than I can count, but suddenly, with everyone looking at me, I froze.

We didn't win that game. Frankly, I didn't inspire a lot of confidence in the people around me on that day. Why? Because I didn't make a clear decision.

It's hard to make decisions. It's even harder to make decisions constantly and harder still to make a fair percentage of those decisions correctly. But without decision, you don't have action, and without action, you don't have outcomes or results. Without those experiences, you can't learn, and if you can't learn, you can't consistently get any better. When you don't make decisions, you'll be stuck going in whichever direction the winds take you.

It's never been easier to start a business than it is today. And it's never been harder to scale or sustain a business against the endless competition of a modern market. The 20th century was all about attaining greater efficiency. The 21st century is about building and expanding adaptability and resilience. And the opportunities of today are calling for you, the decision-makers, to stand up and provide leadership. The only way you do that is by making the decisions, taking the actions, and learning from what you experience.

So, I'm ending this book with a shout out to all the decision-makers out there, big and small; you have my respect. Keep making those decisions. Keep taking those actions.

Keep learning, and the world will be yours for the taking.

RESOURCES

REVENUE OPERATIONS

- Blog—What Is Revenue Operations—https://www.liftenablement.com/revops
- Blog—The Five Levels of Revenue Operations—https://www.liftenablement.com/5-levels
- Blog—What Everybody Is Getting Wrong About Revenue Operations (RevOps) & What You Need To Do About It—https://www.liftenablement.com/whats-wrong-revops

WHY FRAMEWORK IS IMPORTANT

- Blog—Aligning Vectors & Structuring Your Team For Revenue Growth—https://www.liftenablement.com/vectors

THE ECONOMIC MODEL

- Course—Building Your Growth Model For Predictability and Impact—https://growth.liftenablement.com/growth-models

GO-TO-MARKET STRATEGY

- Video—What is Go-to-Market Strategy & How to Define It—https://www.liftenablement.com/gtm-strategy
- Article—Sales Velocity—https://www.liftenablement.com/velocity

MESSAGING, POSITIONING, AND NARRATIVE

- Blog—Move Beyond Thought Leadership to Break The Sales Barrier Myth—https://www.liftenablement.com/pov-insight

SYSTEM DESIGN

- Blog—What Is System Design & Why It's Crucial For Smart Growth—https://www.liftenablement.com/system-design
- Blog—Sisyphus vs. The Flywheel: 5 Tips to Eliminate Friction—https://www.liftenablement.com/sisyphus

THE TECH STACK

- Blog—The Ideal Tech Stack For Mid-Market Companies Serious About Smart Growth—https://www.liftenablement.com/techstack

THE SCOREBOARD

- Video—KPIs Part 1—The What, When, Where & Why of Key Performance Indicators—https://www.liftenablement.com/kpi1
- Video—KPIs Part 2—4 Common Scenarios & Where to Start—https://www.liftenablement.com/kpi2
- Video—The Truth About Sales Quotas—https://www.liftenablement.com/quota

PROCESS

- Video—The JOLT Effect—Interview with Matt Dixon, The Impact of Indecision on Your Sales Efforts—https://www.liftenablement.com/matt-dixon

METHODOLOGY

- Article—The DEALS Framework—https://www.liftenablement.com/deals

EXECUTION AND PERFORMANCE

- Video—Black Line Interview with Steve Pao—https://www.liftenablement.com/steve-pao
- Video—The 3 Zones of Execution—https://www.liftenablement.com/zones

SUCCEEDING WITH REVOPS

- Course—Business Acumen Course—https://www.liftenablement.com/business-acumen
- Video—How to Successfully Launch & Integrate RevOps—https://growth.liftenablement.com/revops

ACKNOWLEDGMENTS

IF I HAD KNOWN HOW DIFFICULT IT WOULD BE TO COMPLETE THIS book, I don't know if I would have had the courage to start.

I've been obsessed my entire adult life with why and how businesses work, what makes them grow, and why people do what they do. *The Revenue Acceleration Framework:*

A Proven Roadmap to Transform and Dynamically Grow Your Business results from this 35-year obsession.

I've decided to keep this section very brief. My first draft was almost four pages of me thanking everyone, and I still thought of people who would legitimately feel left out.

The ideas for this book, let alone the book itself, would not exist were it not for the team I've had the honor of working with at Lift Enablement and the clients we've worked with. While I genuinely want to thank everyone, I am especially grateful for Jess Cardenas. If it weren't for her, I'd still be struggling to find the formula to create the internal magic we've created.

One of the best decisions I've ever made was marrying my wife, Dani. I remember being paralyzed by choice and fear in 2004, shortly after I started the company. If it wasn't for her confidence in me at the time, I doubt this book would be a reality. My son Drew and daughter Dylan have given me decades of inspiration and insights into how and why people do what they do.

I'd be remiss without highlighting the role HubSpot has played in my and Lift's growth as well as the ideas that I share in this book. A special thanks to Brian Halligan and Dharmesh Shah for having the vision and the guts to start such a special company. I will always be appreciative of your responsiveness and openness to feedback, you've inspired me in more ways than I can count. Buck Flather, Barrett King, and Chris Moore, you will always have a special place in my heart. I'm grateful for your insights, your challenge, and your support.

To the team at Scribe, thank you for enabling me to stay focused on what's important and in helping translate my thoughts into something people can understand. And a special shout-out to Janice Bashman.

ABOUT THE AUTHOR

DOUG DAVIDOFF, the founder and CEO of Lift Enablement, has directly advised more than a dozen companies that have sold for a combined value of more than $1 billion.

Doug has decades of experience counseling the leadership of more than 1,500 small and mid-market companies committed to serious growth. He combines an in-depth knowledge of sales and marketing theory and strategy with front-line execution expertise to know what works, what doesn't, and why.

His unique, no-holds-barred approach generates results by integrating real-world experience and research with system design. Doug understands that what's holding most companies back isn't their strategy; it's the chasm between expectations and execution. His proven methods have helped countless companies close that gap.

Doug has authored and co-authored several books, writes the influential *The Demand Creator* blog, co-hosts *The RevOps Show* podcast, and is routinely quoted in major business publications.

A former college baseball coach, he's an avid Nationals and Capitals fan and is always eagerly anticipating his next Springsteen concert. Doug lives in Maryland with his wife and children.

Printed in the USA
CPSIA information can be obtained
at www.ICGtesting.com
LVHW090227300424
778812LV00015B/33/J